The Enchanted World

# MAGICAL JUSTICE

The Enchanted World

# MAGICAL JUSTICE

by the Editors of Time-Life Books

# The Content

Chapter One

## The Code · 6

Chapter Two

# Fortune's Wheel · 56

---

Chapter Three

# The Mediators · 102

Time-Life Books · Alexandria, Virginia

# Chapter One

# THE CODE

There was a time when only a thin skin, unseen and frangible, separated the human realm from the abyss of evil. The pit where monsters lurked and demons cavorted was so close at hand that ordinary mortals could sometimes glimpse its shadows and inhale its poisonous vapors.

Men and women dreaded the prospect of invasion by these forces of chaos. They craved order and harmony; a hierarchy wherein every entity—animal, vegetable, mineral or spiritual—knew its place and obligations. To protect the world from contamination, humans constructed a bulwark of laws governing every aspect of their existence. This code was a safety net woven of many different strands: native kindness and common sense, priestly interpretations of divine will; diktats devised by Kings to keep themselves and their heirs in power; precepts dimly recalled from the days when elder races ruled the earth.

Of far greater antiquity than ink or alphabets, the old laws were passed down through the speech of storytellers and the songs of bards. To inscribe these truths upon the minds of their hearers, the tale-spinners concocted vivid narratives of reward and punishment.

Often, the chief players in these dramas were Kings and Queens. This was, in part, a cunning device to hold the listeners' attention, for what commoner could resist the temptation to glimpse the wonders of treasury, wardrobe and banqueting chamber concealed behind the castle walls? But such stories had a deeper purpose: They brought home the message that no one, however rich in land or absolute in temporal authority, was exempt from moral reckoning.

Yet humble protagonists also had a place in the lore. Their good deeds were gloriously recompensed. Peasants were showered with treasure or elevated from a hovel to a palace. Marriage to a royal spouse was frequently part of the prize.

For the wicked, however, penalties were harsh, ranging from public humiliation to agonizing death. Chilling though these tales of retribution might be, they provided their own consolation, for within their ambit cruelty was always punished, and tyrants were never let off scot-free. If such justice could not be guaranteed in the mundane world, it was, at least, a certainty in the enchanted one.

# The Prodigal Mill

In the old world that gave birth to all lore and legend, no mortal, from the lowliest roadside beggar to the Emperor in his marble palace, was exempt from the obligation to do good and act kindly. But a monarch was born to be a model to his subjects, a living textbook of all the virtues. The very fabric of the universe was threatened when Kings and Queens abused their powers. Yet, being human as well as highborn, they often did, and the chronicles of early ages recounted many well-deserved downfalls and come-uppances of those who wore a crown.

In the long halls of the Norse earls, poets regularly entertained feasters with the salutary tale of the undoing of Frodi, a King who ruled in Denmark in the days when the Vikings were known and feared from Ireland to Byzantium. He had, in the springtime of his reign, been a lucky ruler. His people prospered; their kine waxed fat, their fishing nets were heavy with herring. And, unusual for that turbulent age, they lived in peace. No invading armies menaced their borders, no alien galleys loomed out of the sea, no raiding parties captured their blue-eyed children to sell in distant slave markets.

Indeed, Frodi's only sworn enemy was a King named Mysinger, who nursed a longstanding blood feud, the origins of which were not certain. But Mysinger's kingdom was far away from Denmark, and much too poor to raise an army or a fleet.

Yet Frodi did not share his subjects' contentment. A cankerworm of frustration gnawed at his vitals. Among his store of treasures was an object of inestimable value: a giant mill, consisting of two vast grinding stones, that was reputedly possessed of magic powers. But he could gain no profit or pleasure from it.

Whether the millstones came to him as inheritance, gift or spoil of battle was not recorded. According to rumor, they had been quarried in the Other World and brought to this one on a wind conjured up by weather-working witches. Some claimed they were formed of the lava that poured down the slopes of grim Mount Hekla, the northern gate of hell.

Whatever the truth, they were no ordinary quernstones. Instead of turning wheat or barley into meal, they were said to be capable of grinding out silver, gold, love, happiness or anything their miller asked of them.

But the stones were so heavy that neither Frodi nor the burliest of his earls was strong enough to turn the massive mill. So the device stood idle in Frodi's castle, accumulating dust and legends.

Once, Frodi made a voyage across the cold waters of the Skagerrak to pay a state visit to his cousin, the King of Sweden. Some of the Swedish lord's followers had lately gone a-viking, and Frodi was drinking mead at his cousin's side when they returned with all their booty.

Among the spoils were two items that particularly attracted Frodi's attention: a pair of giantesses, more than ten feet tall, erect as fir trees and broad as bulls. Their cropped hair and coarse tunics of undyed wool marked them as slaves, but their dark eyes glittered with unearthly light. Frodi marveled at their well-muscled

*A Danish King, proud possessor of a set of magic millstones, grew despondent when he could not unlock their powers. If he found a way to make the wheels turn, he could grind out endless supplies of gold and good fortune.*

bulk. If they were not strong enough to turn his magic mill, then nothing was.

The Swedish King, turned maudlin and benevolent by too much mead, offered to make Frodi a gift of the goods that so attracted him, and observed with a wink that his Danish cousin had an eccentric taste in women. Frodi accepted the present with a fulsome speech of gratitude. Then he announced, with a fine semblance of regret, that affairs of state forced him to cut short his visit.

That night, the giantesses, named Menia and Fenia, were bundled into Frodi's own dragon-prowed longship and the convoy sailed. When they landed in Denmark, Frodi led the slaves directly to the massive millstones. Without letting them rest from their journey, or offering them so much as a morsel of barley bread to eat, he ordered them to start grinding.

**W**ell-schooled in obedience, the women began without complaint. Just as Frodi had hoped, they were able to do what no one else in his court had done. Sweating and straining, they grasped the stones, pressed their considerable weight against them and soon they succeeded in turning the enormous rollers. To Frodi's delight, out came all manner of good things for himself and his people: peace, prosperity, fine weather and wealth in endless supply. The more the giantesses produced, the more Frodi wanted. For months he neglected all affairs of state. No edicts were issued by his scribes, no wrongdoers were dragged before him for judgment. All his attention was directed to the delectable dilemma of what to ask the mill for next.

Singing rhythmic chants to spur them in their labors, Menia and Fenia ground without stopping. The sweat poured out of them, almost flooding the chamber. They begged the King to let them pause. But Frodi refused and ordered them to keep working. His voice cracked like a whip across their shoulders. Slaves, he reminded them, lived only to do a master's bidding. He would have them turn the mill as long as it pleased him.

Menia and Fenia may have been giantesses, they may have been more than human, but they were not made of iron. Their massive hands were bleeding and blistered, their necks stiff, their backs nearly broken. They asked again to be allowed a respite. Frodi smiled and said they might stop their labors when the birds stopped singing—but it was the season of nearly endless daylight, the northern summer, and the birdsong never ended. Once more they begged for a rest.

Perhaps because they had been born and bred to slavery, Menia and Fenia were incapable of outright rebellion. The life and wealth of all the realms in the northlands depended on the docility of a vast brigade of slaves and bondmen who stoked the fires, toiled in the fields, spun the yarn and nursed the children. The notion that slaves might defy orders had no means of forming in minds that had been shaped for only one thing: submission. And the two giantesses were no exception. But anger was not beyond them.

The witch-light flickered in their eyes as the same thought came to them at once. If their master wanted them to grind, then grind they must, but they would grind what they pleased. The heavy quern turned slowly and the ponderous millstones grated against one another. But no longer did they turn out gold and worldly goods.

Now Menia and Fenia milled horrors: poverty, pestilence, misery, weapons, war, grief and famine. The two giantesses ground out the plagues that killed sheep and cattle, illnesses that laid low men, violent quarrels that ended with the flash of a knife and a geyser of blood. Droughts from their quern cracked the skin of the Danish earth, floods covered it. Fires glowed dully where barns and houses burned of their own accord, and the keening of mourners at a thousand funerals ululated through the land.

When the King cried out to his two slave-women to stop, the rumble and thunder of their milling drowned out his commands. They were not disobedient; they simply could not hear him.

Then Menia and Fenia ground out a fleet of enemy warships. These were craft built to terrorize peaceable shore-dwellers. Their prows were carved in the form of roaring lions, their sails dyed the color of blood. Rows of spiky oars, like the poisonous spines of sea urchins, thrust out from their sides. To the wonder and puzzlement of the inhabitants, these ships materialized in all the harbors and havens of the kingdom ruled by Mysinger, Frodi's old enemy.

The tale did not explain how Mysinger knew the purpose of this mysterious gift. But he had long been dreaming of the day when he might strike out against the complacent Frodi. He may have felt the warships were the answer to a lifetime of prayers; he may have known of some prophecy, written on rune-stones, that said his moment of glory would come.

Mysinger marshaled his men, calling them away from their stony, infertile fields and their profitless fishing, and stirred them to battle. Bards, at the King's behest, spoke the words of the saga that had preserved for all time the old hates between Frodi's and Mysinger's clans. Then they sang the songs that conjured bloodlust. Hands that had only known the plow or tiller itched for the sword, the spear and the skull-cleaving ax.

Speeded on by favorable winds that the giantesses ground out, the fleet came in good time to Frodi's shore. Under cover of a dense night fog—also the work of the angry millers—the enemy army landed and swooped in a sneak attack.

Many Danes were slaughtered in their beds, many fell fighting; the few survivors were chained up and taken away to be sold as slaves. Frodi himself was struck down by the hand of Mysinger, and died an agonizing death with the sign of the blood eagle hewn out of his back.

While Mysinger's men ransacked the coastal villages, the victorious King entered the castle where Menia and Fenia still strained and labored. The tellers of the tale did not explain how he knew them to be the authoresses of his triumph: Perhaps he saw the shadows of a flashing battle-ax or a burning village

Weary of milling wealth and well-being for their heartless master,
the giantesses Menia and Fenia decided to grind out something
different—weapons, soldiers and warships to equip his lifelong enemy.

emerging from the mill. He announced himself as their new master and commanded them to cease milling. Beaming, they stopped their toil and showered him with thanks. Here was a merciful owner who knew that even slaves needed rest.

Mysinger questioned them at length about the powers of the magic mill. Then he bade them roll their great stones to the sturdiest ship in his fleet.

Menia and Fenia were not allowed to enjoy their leisure for long. Once the galleys put out to sea again, Mysinger decided that he too would use the mill to gain his heart's desire. He was not a wicked King. His first thought was of his country's welfare, and the greatest woe in his land was the lack of salt. Without salt, food gathered in the warm months could not be preserved for the winter. As a result, many families died of starvation. So he ordered Menia and Fenia to set to work again, there on the high seas.

Blessing this new master, who had freed them from the impossible demands of Frodi, the giantesses returned to work with a will. Yet soon they grew tired and asked Mysinger to let them rest.

The King berated them. Had they any idea of the privations caused by the absence of salt? Did they know what it meant to see good fish and flesh rot be-cause there was no way to preserve it? Had they any notion of how his people suffered? Menia and Fenia shrugged and turned again to their labors.

If their new owner wanted salt, then salt he would get. The mill moved under their powerful hands, and the slaves began to grind with an uncanny speed.

Within moments, out came enough salt to preserve all the herrings caught in a year; enough salt to pickle all the rabbit and venison and pig meat on the land; enough salt to weigh down Mysinger's flagship, break its timbers and sink it in the cold gray depths. Without a word of rebellion, Menia and Fenia followed their new lord's orders, and in so doing sent him down to lie forever on the ocean bed, where his bones turned pearly and his head was crowned with seaweed.

**W**hen the galley sank, so did Menia and Fenia, still rotating the mill as the waves closed over their heads. They did what slaves were meant to do; they would work until their master ordered them to stop. But Mysinger was far beyond speaking, and the order never came. The Norse bards said that their mill ground on forever, which was how the waters of all the seas became salt.

With no lord to command them otherwise, Menia and
Fenia continued working even when the millstones sank to the bottom of the sea. Endlessly
turning, they ground out the salt that filled the world's oceans.

# A Harsh Payment in Kind

In the wilderness of Scandinavia lived peoples divided from their neighbors by mountains, forests and deep fjords. This was a land abounding in shape-shifting phantoms, and ordinary folk kept themselves to themselves, knowing it was best not to put too much trust in appearances. Once, the populace of an entire kingdom learned this hard lesson through the sufferings of their young Queen.

The lady had been taken from her real parents in infancy and raised by a fostermother, whose ways and doings were secretive and strange. They lived on the shores of a cold inland sea, in a windowless house with stairways that led nowhere and sinuous corridors with no end.

The old woman sang softly as she did her tasks—whispering into the wind, tracing runic symbols on the empty air, sculpting wax images and flinging them into the tall, tiled stove. Sometimes she vanished for long periods, inexplicably.

The child dwelled placidly inside a thicket of rules and restrictions: Certain rooms were out of bounds, certain words were forbidden. But as she grew up, she began to chafe against these prohibitions. One day her fostermother announced that she was going on a long journey; as always, she forbade the girl to open the three doors on the top storey.

But this time the fosterling rebelled. She began to wonder what secrets her guardian wished to keep from her. She paced back and forth before the doors a hundred times, then impulsively opened one. With a rush of wind and a flash of light, a shooting star escaped, skittered down the twisting corridor and vanished into the night. Terrified, the girl banged the door shut. Bent double with cramps, she awaited her guardian's return.

Once home, the fostermother knew, without asking, what had happened. She made the girl's ears ring with a severe scolding. When the time came for another journey, she raised an admonitory finger and said only, "Once warned."

Alone again, the girl decided that a scolding was a small price to pay for satisfying her curiosity. When she opened the second door, a great white moon rolled out, then melted into the empty air. When the fostermother returned, her face was as pale as the missing moon, but she said nothing until mysterious business called her from home again. She pointed toward the banned portals, murmured the words "Twice warned," and was gone.

The girl's fingers itched to grasp the cut-crystal doorknob of the third room. Moments after her guardian's departure, she pushed the third door open. A golden orb, so hot and bright it could only be the sun, exploded in her face and disappeared in a shower of hissing sparks. Its fiery afterimage was still glowing inside her eyelids when she felt a sharp tap on her shoulder. The old woman was back.

"Thrice warned," she hissed, grim faced. She lamented the loss of her treasures, last relics of a world of glory that lay beyond the ken of mortals. There was only one fitting punishment. Raising her voice in an uncanny howl, she sang the maiden's speech away and sent her out into the world, a silent traveler.

*A young Queen was found besmeared with the blood of her infant child, who had vanished. The deed was the work of a mysterious crone, settling an old score.*

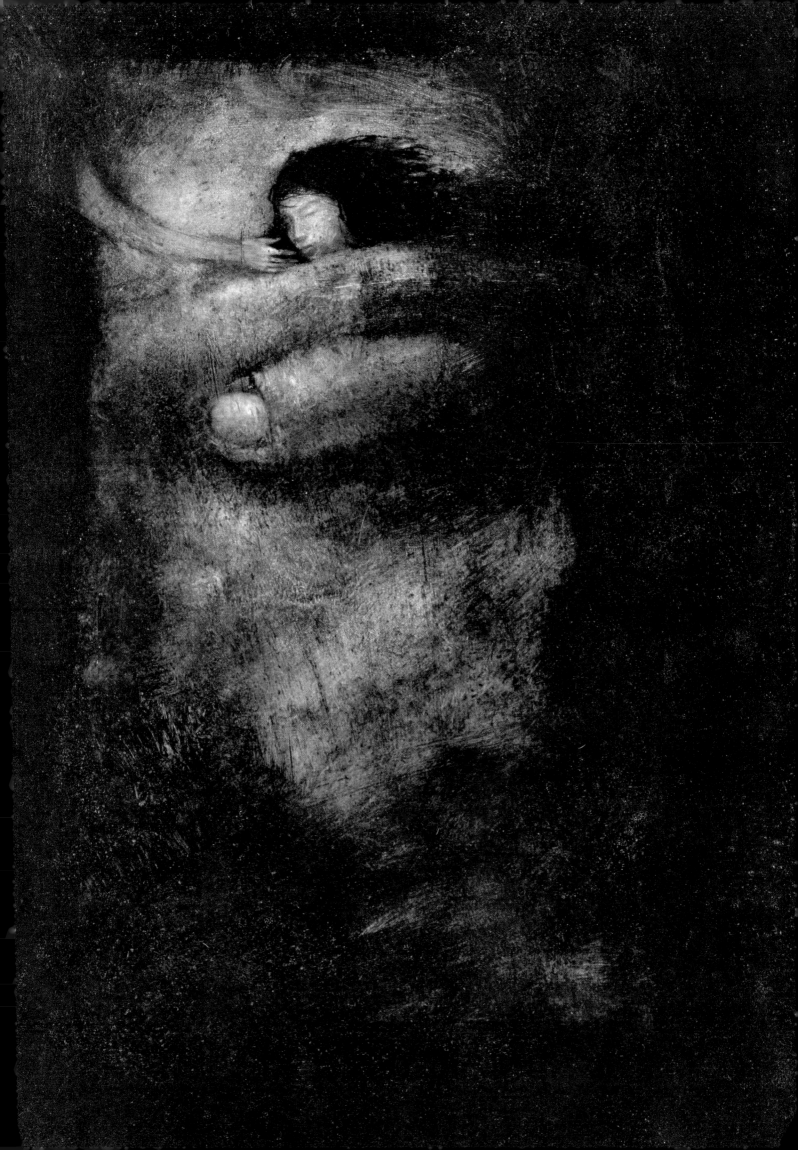

But before the girl had walked many miles she met a young King, out hunting deer. Smitten by her beauty and undeterred by her mysterious muteness, he asked her to be his Queen. King though he might have been, his wooing was like any other man's; it was not the manner of their marriage but its outcome that made the tale so remarkable. The monarch's mother was appalled by the match, and hinted that the maid had something sinister about her. When the royal couple's first child was born, the Queen Mother's suspicions seemed to be confirmed, for on its first day of life the baby disappeared. The only trace was a bloodstain on the young Queen's mouth, a sure sign of sorcery. It was well known that witches craved the flesh of human infants.

The Queen, unable to speak in her own defense, could tell no one what had happened. The King refused to believe that his wife had eaten their first-born and insisted that it had been stolen by some enemy of the crown. When a second child was awaited, he ordered dozens of guards to patrol the palace, to watch over the newborn heir. After she gave birth, the Queen heard a strange high-pitched chanting echo through the palace, saw her attendants fall into a stupor, then lost consciousness herself. Once again, the dawn revealed the mother's empty arms and bloody mouth. The King insisted that so beautiful a face could never conceal a witch's heart. If there were evil magic about, it had been perpetrated by other hands.

When the Queen was brought to bed a third time, the King ordered the infant's cradle to be wrapped in chains of iron, a metal abhorrent to races not quite human. Again, precautions were useless: The guards slept and the chains were soundlessly severed. But the Queen remained awake, bound by a spell that left her helpless. Only her eyes moved, following the progress of a hooded shape through the barricaded door and across the chamber. It was her fostermother. The old woman pricked the baby's finger and smeared its mother's mouth with blood. "Fair payment," she said, "for the three treasures you took from me." Then she vanished with the infant.

The Queen knew the King would no longer be able to protect her. This time, the Queen Mother's accusations were heeded, and the King had to sign the death warrant. A pyre was made ready in the marketplace and the Queen tied to a stake. But before the faggots could be lit, the old woman appeared, leading two stolen princelings and carrying the third.

The crowd parted. No one could mistake the eerie light in the crone's eyes: She was one of the elder race who had formerly ruled the earth, and still retained formidable power. She told the tale of the young girl's disobedience and the loss of the three treasures. Only when her fosterdaughter had endured an equal agony was forgiveness possible. Now the crime was expiated. So saying, the old woman handed over the three children to the weeping King. He motioned the guards to release his wife, then turned again to address the crone. But she had vanished.

## The King of Beasts returns a favor

In a world where every tree might harbor a nymph, the smallest act of cruelty to another living thing could incur a savage vengeance; the simplest kindness, on the other hand, could win unforeseen rewards. Sages cited the salutary tale of Androcles—a slave who showed bloodthirsty Rome the value of compassion. It happened so:

No longer able to bear his brutal master's thrashings, Androcles one day slipped his chains and escaped. He sprinted through the streets of Rome, out the city's great gate, across the surrounding fields and on into the forest. At last he collapsed, exhausted, at the mouth of a cave.

When he sat up, Androcles was horrified to see a massive lion emerging from the cavern. The animal slowly approached him, then placed a huge, bleeding paw in his lap. Protruding from the matted fur was a jagged thorn. A sudden flood of pity for the animal drowned the slave's fear. Firmly grasping the wounded paw, he drew out the barb and showed it to the lion. At once, the beast turned and stalked away.

After wandering far and enduring many hardships, Androcles was recaptured and returned to Rome. The punishment he faced for his attempted escape was to fight unarmed with a starving lion in Rome's palace of bloodshed—the arena.

From his cell under the stands, Androcles could hear the roars of the hungry beasts in their pen. Then the guards thrust him out before the chanting crowds to meet his executioner. But, through some extraordinary quirk of fate, the lion was the very same animal that Androcles had tended in the cave. Though maddened with hunger, the great cat recognized its gentle friend and lay down at his feet like a dog. The crowd was shocked into silence. Challenged to explain his magic, the slave told his tale, moving the Emperor to set him free.

# The Dutiful Daughter

In the Orient, the qualities that were most highly prized in women were obedience and humility. Whatever her social status, any girl or woman who hewed to these virtues without wavering might receive miraculous rewards. A story from old Japan held up a young peasant girl as an example of this truth.

As the only daughter of aged parents, the girl was accustomed to hardship. She was wage earner, housekeeper, cook and nurse, and each night she fell into an exhausted slumber the moment she lay down. But to her parents she was doubly precious: Not only was she their only support, but she was also of a rare beauty unmatched in their neighborhood. Such loveliness, as her mother well knew, had its attendant dangers.

In time, the girl's father died and her mother's anxiety increased. She observed the glances directed at her daughter by the village boys, and, being a pious woman and aware that she too would not survive much longer on this earth, she resolved on a plan to safeguard her daughter's virtue. One evening she took from the kitchen a plain lacquered bowl and placed it on her daughter's head, carefully tucking beneath its rim every strand of the girl's fine hair. Never, she instructed, was the girl to remove this bowl.

*Obedient to her mother's dying wish, a Japanese peasant girl covered her head with a wooden bowl to shield her beauty from the gaze of lustful men.*

Not long afterward, the mother died. Working alone in the rice fields, the girl became a figure of fun: Children threw pebbles at the bowl clamped to her head, and the boys of her own age soon turned their attentions elsewhere. But she toiled steadily on down row after muddy row, plucking the ripened grass with her agile, long-fingered hands until the sun sank below the horizon and her shadow merged with darkness.

At last the harvest was over, and the rice fields were bare beneath a wintry sky that seemed to mirror her own future. Without work, and without a family to provide a marriage dowry for her, how could she go on supporting herself? But her diligence had not gone unnoticed. As she returned to her empty home, she was approached by the wealthy farmer who owned the rice fields. His wife was ill,

he explained; he had no daughters, and he needed domestic help.

The girl's housekeeping skills now came into their own. From dawn until sunset she never stopped work: rolling up the sleeping mats, sweeping the floors, preparing the meals and decorating the farmer's mansion with tasteful arrangements of flowers. Indeed, only one month after her arrival, when the farmer's young son returned home from the capital city of Kyoto to see his ailing mother, she was already an indispensable member of the household.

The boy's parents were happy to be reunited with their intelligent and handsome son, but they sensed that he would soon grow bored with their provincial ways and return to Kyoto where his studies had prepared him for an excellent career. However, the boy was intrigued by the new maidservant. He realized that country girls were more conservative in their habits than his Kyoto companions,

but for a girl to wear a bowl on her head seemed to him to be taking modesty to a ridiculous extreme.

Aided by the girl's skillful nursing, the farmer's wife was soon fully recovered again. But the girl stayed on—and so, to his parents' surprise, did their son. Observing the girl going about her household duties, the boy had become aware that his initial curiosity was developing into a stronger attraction. As the girl glided silently from room to room, the boy would attempt to engage her in conversation and to see more closely under the bowl she wore on her head.

One day, the boy went to his father and declared his intentions: He wished to marry the girl. His father was prepared to agree, but his mother could see no sense in the match. After all, the girl was only a household servant and would bring no dowry. And there was also the matter of the bowl: Surely it must hide some dreadful disfigurement, since no pretty girl would conceal her attractions in this way.

When the boy remained insistent, his father suggested that he put his proposal to the girl herself. She refused at once, aware that such a marriage would cause dissension in the household and would be poor repayment for the kindness this family had shown her. And she remained quite steadfast against the boy's repeated pleas—until, one night, she heard in her sleep the voice of her mother. The mother said that she could not have wished for a more dutiful daughter, but now, for the first time in her life, the girl must follow the dictates of her own heart and accept the boy's proposal.

The boy was filled with delight, and his father also was pleased. But as the preparations for the wedding proceeded, the boy's mother became increasingly uneasy. It was bad enough that her son should be marrying a servant, but that the girl should be wearing a kitchen bowl in front of all the guests and relations— this was too much to bear.

The girl was anxious to please her future mother-in-law, and on the morning of the wedding she attempted to remove the bowl from her head. She pulled and tugged, and a strange groaning sound seemed to be caused by her efforts, but the bowl would not come off. The boy tried to comfort his bride, assuring her that the bowl was no impediment to his love, and they walked forward together to meet the assembled guests.

The climax of the wedding was the traditional ceremony known as "three times three." While the boy's father was preparing the first cup of sake, which would be sipped three times by both bride and groom and then followed by more cups, the guests were whispering among themselves and laughing at the strange appearance of the bride; but when the cup was filled, everyone was respectfully silent. The girl took the cup and raised it to her lips—and suddenly, with a startling noise, the bowl upon her head split apart, spilling gold and silver and countless precious stones. All who witnessed were dazzled by the girl's beauty and by the dowry won through her humility.

*A rich young farmer, undeterred by his friends' mockery, married the penniless girl whose face he had never seen. On their wedding day, the bowl broke of its own accord, bringing an unexpected dowry.*

# The Waters of Hell and Heaven

Uttered on a deathbed, parental wishes carried tremendous power. In the same tradition as the tale of the young Japanese maiden was another legend from half a world away, relating the wonders made known to Haninah, a young scholar in ancient Palestine.

Haninah's father was a mystic, able to read the future like a book. When he saw the Angel of Death on his threshold, he summoned his son to say farewell. He issued one last command: After his death, when the prescribed week of mourning was over, Haninah was to go to the marketplace and buy the first thing he saw there. If it turned out to be a living creature, Haninah must nourish and cherish it as if it were his kin.

When the time came, Haninah went to the bazaar and purchased the first item he set eyes upon—a silver jar. When he took the vessel home and opened it, a frog jumped out, danced and skittered wildly around the room, then bounded back into the jar again.

Haninah consulted many books to determine what foods frogs liked best, and he fed the creature so generously that it was soon too big for its container. He then built it a cabinet of fragrant cedarwood, but it was not long before the ever-fatter frog outgrew this second home. Sparing no expense, Haninah ordered a new room to be built onto his house. The carpenters laughed when they learned his purpose, but Haninah seemed oblivious to the joke.

Finally he was forced to confess to the frog that he had no money left to feed it. He nearly fainted from shock when the creature addressed him in perfectly grammatical Aramaic—Haninah's native tongue. The frog announced it was no common amphibian, but a shape-shifting spirit, that now proposed to return Haninah's kindness. It offered the scholar anything he desired.

So learned and pious a youth as Haninah knew that miracles were possible. It was a measure of his virtue that he asked only one thing: a better understanding of the sacred texts and the holy law.

The frog hopped away and returned with a piece of paper, inscribed with multicolored charms and sacred symbols. He bade Haninah swallow the sheet. With it, Haninah would ingest a perfect knowledge of the law, together with an understanding of the seventy spoken tongues of humankind and all the languages of birds and beasts.

With this new learning, Haninah's scholarly reputation soared. Even the King, a capricious, hot-tempered tyrant, consulted him on obscure points of law.

In spite of the honors that were heaped upon him, Haninah continued to live simply. His linguistic skills enabled him to enjoy many enlightening conversations with birds and animals. One morning, two ravens flew across his path and screamed a warning of impending danger. Haninah was mystified; he had no enemies that he knew of.

That day he was summoned to the palace. The King held up a long, glistening golden hair, imbued with a faint aura of attar of roses, and asked Haninah what he

*At a market in old Jerusalem, a scholar purchased a jar that concealed a frog.*
*But the creature proved to be no ordinary amphibian,*
*and it repaid its owner's kindness with gifts of occult knowledge.*

made of it. Peering at the long strand, Haninah remarked that he had heard of golden-haired people, but not in Palestine. The King explained that it had dropped from the beak of a bird flying through the palace gardens.

There was no doubt, declared the monarch, that this was a woman's hair. He wanted its owner for his wife. He had always spurned his counselor's pleas to secure the kingdom's future by marrying and begetting heirs. Never before had he found a woman he wanted to wed. Now, perversely, his passion was aroused by this inaccessible golden stranger.

He commanded the all-wise Haninah to find her. If he failed to do so, he would die, and all the other scholars of Palestine with him. Haninah knew this threat had substance. The current reign was infamous for summary executions on trumped-up charges. So he set out on a solitary search for the woman with hair like the sun. The birds, which were great exchangers of travelers' tales and gossip, told him of a country that was ruled by a yellow-haired Queen. To meet his modest needs on the journey, he carried three loaves of bread and a purse containing twelve ducats.

On the first day of his travels, he heard the lamentations of a hungry raven, complaining that the land was devoid of the worms and grubs it lived on. Without hesitation, Haninah shared one of his loaves with the bird. The next day, he encountered a dog, mangy and miserable, that had been driven away from the house of its master. Haninah gave the dog the last of his bread. He had, after all, twelve ducats to buy provisions. But then he saw some fishermen netting a giant salmon. Because he could not bear to see the magnificent fish suffer, he purchased it on the spot, for twelve ducats, then tossed it back into the sea.

Then he came to the land ruled by the golden-haired lady. Granted an audience, he asked the Queen if the single strand was hers. She admitted that a bird had plucked a hair from her head not long before. So Haninah presented the King's proposal; he spoke of the considerable political advantages to be gained by the union, and described the massacre of scholars that would ensue if she declined.

The Queen, who was as learned in her own way as Haninah, said she would wed the King, but only if his ambassador would carry out two missions for her. First, Haninah was to fetch her two jugs of water—one from heaven and one from hell. Haninah went into the wilderness and wept at the impossibility.

But the raven he had fed came to him and offered to help. It flew away over the horizon and soon returned with a jar hooked to each wing, one filled with fouled and boiling water, the other with a cool, clear liquid.

The Queen put the water to the test. She splashed a little hell-water on her hand, and shrieked when it burned her, then healed the pain at once by bathing the wound in the liquor of heaven. Satisfied, she sent Haninah on his second quest. She asked him to find a jeweled signet ring that she had lost in the sea.

Haninah walked by the shore, praying aloud for some miracle, when the salmon he had rescued leaped out of the waves. Learning of Haninah's plight, it swam off to the court of the monster, Leviathan, Lord of the Waters, who commanded his subjects to reveal the ring's whereabouts. Then a small fish appeared and coughed up the ring it had inadvertently swallowed. But before Haninah could return the ring to the Queen, a wild boar charged out of the forest, knocked Haninah down and made off with it. Haninah cursed the boar, for he knew that wild swine were beloved of the Devil, who would be delighted to see the holy men of Palestine slaughtered. Then he reproved himself for the sin of despair, and was only a little surprised to see the dog he had saved from starvation loping after the boar. Covering his ears to shut out the sounds of mayhem, Haninah sent up thankful prayers. The dog soon trotted up, bearing the ring in its blood-flecked mouth.

As promised, the Queen accompanied Haninah back to Palestine, passing the journey in learned conversation and debate. The King was delighted with his bride, and loud in his praises of Haninah. But, as he made his way home from the palace, Haninah was set upon by an unknown assailant—possibly an envious courtier—and murdered. As soon as the alarm was raised, the Queen came running up with the two jars of heavenly and hellish water. She gently anointed the corpse with a little of the celestial liquid, and the scholar, to the astonishment of the multitude, rose up hale again. Blinking, he murmured of the wonders of paradise. The King would not rest until he too had been killed and resurrected. He demanded that his bride repeat the miracle. She prevaricated, explaining that Haninah had only been revived because he was a truly good man. Unless the King's soul was equally pure, she warned against the adventure.

The tyrant glowered and accused her of favoring Haninah. Seeing murder in his eye, she shrugged and flung the jar of hell-water over him. He was instantly reduced to a little pyramid of dust and ashes. She cast the water of heaven over the heap and nothing happened. Awed by the Queen's power, and respectful of Haninah, the royal counselors persuaded them to marry each other and share the crown of Palestine in the tyrant's place.

After the scholar was slain by an unknown assailant, his lips were moistened with water brought from heaven. The awestruck crowd waited to see if this divine liquor would restore his life.

Long-memoried tale-spinners of the Caucasus recalled the days when the foxes roaming the mountain meadows and forests above the Caspian Sea possessed powers of speech and more than a human measure of wit. They were ruthless, shrewd, but fiercely loyal to those who befriended them.

Once a miller named Lause-Hadschi caught a fox among his chickens. The hens were the miller's only wealth, and he raised his cudgel high over the thief's back. Spitting out a mouthful of feathers, the fox begged for mercy, promising the man great riches in return. Thinking of his bare larder, his thin cloak and the long winter ahead, the miller lowered his cudgel. The fox assured him there was honor among animals. He would not break his promise. Casting a worried glance at his surviving poultry, the miller hesitated, then let the creature go. The fox ran down the road, until his eye was caught by a half-buried silver coin. He gazed at it for a long moment, summoning up all the ancient cunning of his race. Then, hiding the coin in his fur, he trotted boldly up to the Governor's palace, where he introduced himself as the Grand Vizier of the Lord Bukutschichan. The fox explained that his master was a foreign potentate who was presently on a visit to the neighborhood. He wished to

count his heaps of silver, but some stupid servant had forgotten to pack the scoop specially reserved for this purpose. Perhaps the Governor would kindly lend him one? The Governor complied. The fox inserted the coin into a crack in the scoop and returned the implement to the Governor three days later, explaining it had taken his master that long to count the coins. The old man found the silver piece in the scoop and thought that Bukutschichan must indeed be a wealthy lord.

The next day, the fox obtained a gold coin—whether by luck or thievery the story did not say—and again borrowed the scoop. This time Bukutschichan wished to count his gold When the Governor shook the scoop on its return, a coin dropped out. Dazzled by the apparent size of the stranger's fortune, he asked the fox to offer Bukutschichan his daughter in marriage. A rendezvous was agreed for the next day, at the ford of the river flowing beyond the palace gate.

At the mill, meanwhile, Lause-Hadschi bent low under heavy sacks of other men's grain. He had not seen the fox for a week, and if he thought of that scoundrel at all, it was merely to call himself a fool for letting such vermin escape.

It was only Lause-Hadschi's weariness which stayed his hand when the fox appeared by the millrace. Laughing at the story of the silver and gold, the Governor and his daughter, he asked the fox why he should believe this incredible tale.

The fox in turn asked why, having nothing to lose, the miller should not

31

*By a cruel deception, the fox caused a dragon's death, and appropriated its lands and castle for his master's use.*

believe it. Lause-Hadschi, thrusting calloused hands into empty pockets, could only agree. Yet how could he, a simple man clad in threadbare fustian, introduce himself as the noble Bukutschichan?

The fox led the miller to a meadow carpeted with mountain flowers, where he gathered every perfect bloom and wove a rich brocade of blossoms. Finally, he lay across the miller's shoulders a mantle of blue forget-me-nots, purple violets, pink phlox and white anemones. Then he fashioned a rough sword from pale limewood and gave it to Lause-Hadschi, telling him to ford the river at noon wearing only his robe and sword.

The fox crossed the river at once to await the Governor's party. They arrived just before midday and the fox called out to them, heralding his master's approach on the far bank. Across the river they saw the noble Bukutschichan, wrapped in a garment of brilliant hue and carrying a sword that gleamed like silver in the sun.

But when he waded into the river, the current swept his finery away. Naked and shivering, Bukutschichan climbed up the riverbank. The Governor himself offered the lord his own fine coat, though he feared it was but a shabby replacement for the magnificent robe that was lost.

The party escorted Bukutschichan to the palace. Amazed by its grandeur, the miller said not a word, while the fox explained that his master's surprise at finding so simple a residence had silenced him. But, he added, the Governor's daughter was certainly beautiful enough

to make Bukutschichan a fitting wife, despite her obviously humble upbringing.

The Governor married them at once, before Bukutschichan could change his mind, and arranged a retinue of soldiers and servants to accompany them to the great lord's estate. The fox told the outriders to wait a day, explaining that he must hurry ahead to make preparations.

The creature raced away and ran until he reached a fruitful valley of rich fields and fat flocks. He asked a shepherd who owned the farms and forests and learned that a terrible dragon was lord of the valley. There was nothing strange in this, for once dragons had held sway over all the earth, and in these remote mountain regions they were still to be found.

The fox announced that an army led by seven tyrant Kings was coming to lay waste the land. If the shepherd would save his own life, the fox warned, he must tell the invaders that noble Bukutschichan

ruled the land, for his was the only name feared by the seven kings.

The fox traveled through the valley, telling the same tale to all. At last he came to the dragon's castle. The monster, whose cruelty was only exceeded by its cowardice, had heard rumors of the army on the march. The fox found it looking for a place to hide, and counseled the creature to conceal itself in a haystack. When the monster was buried in the hay, the fox quickly set it alight and roasted the dragon alive.

The fire was still burning when the wedding party arrived. Along the way, every farmer, herdsman and dairymaid had named Bukutschichan as lord of their valley. And indeed, the great castle with its rich treasury and its wide demesne stood empty, waiting for Bukutschichan.

# Purgation in the wilderness

The early Hebrew sages told how a hard lesson in the virtues of humility was learned by one of the mightiest Kings of ancient Babylon. This monarch had transformed his capital into the queen of cities by adorning it with splendid temples, ziggurats and gardens. He never stopped boasting about his works.

One night he had a strange and alarming dream. In it he stood beside a towering tree whose top touched the sky. Birds nested in the branches and animals sheltered down below. Suddenly a messenger from heaven appeared and ordered that the tree be cut down and the proud King exiled from the society of humans, to live like an ox in the fields.

Upon awakening, the King recounted the vision to his master magician. This venerated interpreter of dreams warned that it was the King himself who would be felled and exiled if he did not learn to act more humbly. A year passed and the King duly forgot the prophecy. One day, as he strutted about his palace basking in the flattery of the court nobles, a volley of thunder shook the skies, and the King heard what seemed to him to be a voice announcing that his reign was over. It drove him mad.

The monarch no longer knew where or what he was. He rushed out to the fields, where he went on all fours like a wild beast, chewing the grass and bellowing at passersby. Drenched by dew and dirtied by mud, the King's hair grew long and matted. His hands and feet were torn by stones and thorns. After seven months of this bestial existence, the monarch finally understood the error of his former ways. Repentant, he stood upright and staggered home. Weeping tears of joy, relief and shame, he found his throne still waiting. But he was a different man than the arrogant monarch who had left it, and proved it by ruling with greater wisdom and humility.

# Raiment beyond Compare

In the days when Emperors ruled as the earthly regents of the gods, they were responsible for the welfare of their people. As recounted in an old legend, however, there was once an Emperor who was so proud and vain that he cared for nothing in his realm except his wardrobe. Crops might rot on the ground and bandits roam freely in the provinces, but who cared about such details when the Emperor looked so fine? For walking in the palace gardens he wore one suit of apparel, for receiving his Chamberlain another, for taking refreshment another—and so it went on, each day a continuous parade of the most sumptuous costumes.

Naturally, weavers and cloth-makers from many lands flocked to the court of this most generous patron. One day two strangers arrived who desired to make the Emperor a costume of unparalleled beauty. The clothes they made, they claimed, could be appreciated only by the most discerning clients; indeed, so delicate was their workmanship that to dishonest persons and those of low intelligence the clothes remained wholly invisible. The Emperor could not refuse. How handsome he would look—and how useful it would be to discover who among his retainers was unworthy to serve him.

News of the wonderful properties of the Emperor's new clothes spread rapidly. From morning till night, a crowd of excited citizens stood gossiping on the sidewalk beneath the strangers' room, gazing in astonishment at the reels of gossamer silk thread and bales of costly yarn that the Emperor sent from the palace. Even the Emperor could hardly contain his curiosity, and he sent his Chamberlain to view the work in progress.

The strangers received the Chamberlain hospitably and asked his opinion of what he saw. This was a difficult question, since what the Chamberlain saw was an empty loom with all the treadles, heddles, uprights and cross-beams as they should be, but with not a thread upon it. He was about to demand an explanation, but then he remembered the strangers' claim—that their work could not be perceived by dimwits and scoundrels.

One of the strangers took the Chamberlain's hand and asked him to feel for himself the fine texture of the material. "Very fine indeed," said the Chamberlain, feeling nothing at all, and he admired the geometric patterns, all picked out in rare dyes that would never fade. Then he hurried back to tell the Emperor before he could forget a single detail.

Highly pleased, the Emperor sent his Treasurer to confirm the report. He, too, saw neither warp nor weft, not a scrap of woven cloth; but he was a clever man, not unhappy in his lucrative job, so he declared himself hugely impressed.

Now the Emperor decided he must see for himself. Accompanied by his most trusted officials, he arrived at the strangers' lodging and walked eagerly up the stairs. As the door opened, the Chamberlain and the Treasurer exclaimed in wonder. Had they not been right, they asked, to praise the cloth so highly? And everyone agreed that the Emperor must wear this costume in the following

Two craftsmen promised a vainglorious Emperor clothing of unparalleled
magnificence but invisible to fools and traitors. The Chamberlain, sent
by the Emperor to inspect the work, was loud and lavish in his praises.

week's procession; no other would do.

Then the courtiers stood back to allow the Emperor to approach the loom more closely—so close, in fact, that he could have stretched out his hand through the space where the cloth should have been. He walked slowly round the loom, bending his head to look from every angle and narrowing his eyes in concentration. At last, he nodded the imperial assent.

With only a week to finish the clothes, the strangers worked feverishly. More yarn, more spun-silk fiber, more precious sequins were delivered daily, together with spiced dishes from the palace kitchens to revive their energy. Throughout the final night a light shone from the upstairs window, and a hushed crowd below listened to the rapid snipping of scissors and the rattle of the shuttle across the loom.

Five minutes before the Emperor arrived with his courtiers on the morning of the procession, the snipping and rattling finally ceased. Item by item, the strangers held up their work for approval: garments so soft and well cut that the wearer would not even feel them; the high-collared tunic with embroidered cuffs; the fur-lined mantle; and the long, long train which would require no less than ten servants to hold it off the ground.

The Emperor stripped down to his underwear and was fitted with his new attire. A tall mirror was held up so that he could examine the finished effect: the front view, with his chest puffed out and head raised at a noble angle; then the right profile, the left profile, and finally, peering over his shoulder, the rear view, with the deep folds of the train cascading to the floor. Then trumpets blared to announce the start of the procession.

The entire population of the city—all discerning people, not a single knave or fool—gasped in admiration, then broke into loud applause. Of the Emperor's thousand costumes, this was undoubtedly the finest. They climbed to the rooftops to gain a better view. Those at the back of the crowd—among them a small boy—clambered up onto each other's shoulders or pressed eagerly forward.

Elbowing and pushing his way, the young boy at last broke through to the front. He stared, looked up at his cheering neighbors, and stared again. And then: "But he's got *nothing on!*"

Those who heard were suddenly silent, then whispered in confusion: "Nothing on? What does the boy mean, 'nothing on?' That's the Emperor out there!" And they looked again, and ripples of amusement began to spread steadily outward from around the boy's head.

With his hands clenched by his sides, his nose held high and gales of laughter thundering in his ears, the almost-naked Emperor was compelled to walk on to the very end of the procession. His head swam with furious plans for revenge—but by now the two wily strangers were nowhere to be found. Some people said they had hurried out the city gates with their booty; others insisted they had vanished back to the realm of the gods, whence they had come as avenging angels. For they were never seen on earth again.

*Proud of garments so fine that only loyal subjects could see them,
the Emperor displayed them in a procession of great pomp and ceremony.*

# The Beggar's Bride

It was a sad truth that, in the age of courtly love, marriages among the highest born were rarely affairs of the heart. Dynastic politics, rather than natural affection, led brides to the altar. Yet in a ducal palace in the Rhineland there lived a rebellious young woman who could not reconcile her duty to family and country with her dreams of finding the passionate love that minstrels sang of.

She scandalized the court when, against all the strategic and economic interests of the country, she refused an alliance with a Prince she had never seen. She insisted that, if she could not marry a partner of her own choosing, she would die a virgin. The Duke, angry at her disobedience, announced that he would marry his daughter to the first stranger who came along.

The palace was full of spies, and word of the Duke's declaration soon reached the ears of the rejected nobleman. He, like the Duke's daughter, was a sentimental dreamer. The lady herself attracted him almost as much as her powerful dynastic connections.

Disguising himself as a beggar, the nobleman hurried to the court to claim his reluctant bride, and duly married her. When they left the palace, her lesson in the realities of love began.

The beggar took his new wife on a footsore journey back to his own country—the same land she would have ruled if she had married the man of her father's choice. For one brought up in a palace, life in a hovel was a nightmare, and at first the young woman mourned all that she had lost.

Little by little she came to love the beggar, for he was warm and tender by night, making her forget the day's toil. Yet he was often absent from home, seeking alms or employment.

She tried to please her husband by making herself useful, but every attempt failed. Her hands were too delicate for any work; even spinning made her soft fingers bleed. She was successful, for a while, at selling coarse pots in the marketplace, but one day, a drunken hussar rode recklessly among her goods, reducing them to a scattered mass of shards and destroying her trade.

Finally, she was reduced to service as a kitchen maid in the palace of the lord she should have married. On her second day at work in the steaming scullery, word came down that the master wanted the new servant—no one else would do—to attend him at table. What she saw when she entered the tapestried hall made her drop her platter of roasted venison with a crash, sending rivulets of gravy across the marble floor.

For the nobleman was her own husband. He had exchanged his ragged homespun garments for rich purple robes trimmed with miniver and sable. He explained that he had disguised himself as a mendicant in order to win her hand and now adored her all the more because she loved him for himself, not for his wealth. The powers that guide lovers had rewarded her for being obedient to a dream: She was allowed to be true both to her heart and to her homeland.

*When a drunken hussar shattered the pots at her stall, the market trader's meager livelihood was ruined. Unbeknown to the crowd, she was a once-proud Princess, forced into marriage with a mendicant to learn humility.*

# A Quest for Expiation

The ancient lore of justice encompassed moral dilemmas as well as absolutes of right and wrong. One particularly gray area was that of repentance. What actions, if any, could expiate a life of crime? A tale from the Slavic lands provided a surprising answer.

It concerned the ferocious chieftain of a band of thieves, who one day came across a book of holy scriptures. That night, while the rest of the gang gnawed on the bones of stolen sheep and sang bawdy ballads in an off-key chorus, the robber-king huddled by the camp fire, reading accounts of ancient battles, miracles and magic. His attention never wandered, even when the text moved from chronicles of wonders to discourses on good and evil.

The very act of reading changed him. When next he raised his cudgel to club a victim, he heard the words of the book in his ear, commanding him not to kill. He saw a vision of his own shriveled soul consumed by hellfire.

Abruptly, he told his band to choose another chieftain. He sought out the cave of a hermit priest, well known in the district, and begged forgiveness. The cowled recluse listened without comment to a catalog of crimes; the recitation began before sunset and ended after dawn.

The holy man declared the thief had only one hope for redemption: He was to retire into the forest, take the cudgel with which he had battered so many victims and plant it in the earth. Then he was to go on hands and knees to a distant stream, obtain a mouthful of water, crawl back to the cudgel and moisten it with the liquid. If the weapon turned to living wood again and sprouted leaves, it would be a sign that he was forgiven.

The penitent did as the hermit ordered. For years, he crawled half naked from stream to cudgel and back again, until his beard swept the ground before him and time had no measure or meaning.

One day, the penitent wept tears of ecstasy. His cudgel displayed a few tentative green shoots. He set off for the stream with renewed vigor, praying that his ordeal was nearly ended. As he approached the bank, he heard two men's voices. Shy of human contact after so long a solitude, he hid behind a bush.

Their conversation, as they lolled by the stream, made it plain to him that they were informers, paid by despotic landlords to report any rebellious talk among the peasants. The pair were chuckling over the punishments meted out to the families they accused: the adults flogged to death with knouts, the orphans driven off the manors to starve.

The penitent quaked with wrath. His own crimes paled beside these. He seized a great stone, rushed out from the bush and battered the spies to death.

Then he crawled back, heartsore, to his cudgel, fearing this one rash act had undone all his years of repentance. Yet he knew his deed had prevented bloodshed on a far greater scale. Those powers that watched over humankind must have concurred, for when he reached the cudgel he saw it had quickened into life and was now festooned with leaves and blossoms.

## The trees' perpetual penance

There was a time, said the old Danish bards, when all trees stayed forever green, keeping their leaves even in the hardest winter. In those days every living thing, whether plant or animal, had a soul and an individual character, and none was exempt from the moral code. Even trees were expected to show kindness to their fellow creatures and might be punished for a cruel deed.

The stage for just such a punishment was set, late one September, when flocks of garrulous redwings gathered in their thousands for their migratory flight from the advancing winter. As the sun set, they began the arduous journey that would take them over the waters of the Mediterranean and the sands of the Sahara to the warm lands of Africa. But one was left behind, unable to fly because its wing was broken.

The injured bird hopped and fluttered from tree to tree, seeking shelter from the coming cold. A birch tree swayed in a dance with the wind and took no heed of the bird's request. Neither did the willow, nursing some deep and secret sorrow as it drooped mournfully over a stream. And the proud oak, soaring skyward, did not deign to notice the redwing at its feet.

At last the weary bird came to a spruce, tallest of the forest trees, which received him charitably and drew its thick-growing needles tight round him. A pine nearby spread its branches wide to shelter the creature more closely, and a dark juniper offered an abundance of berries to feed the bird until better days.

The birch, the willow and the oak paid for their inhospitality. When the wind howled after the first frosts, it stripped them naked and shook them from their dreams.

Forever after, they would be vulnerable to winter's blasts and face the snows as shivering skeletons, while the kinder spruce, pine and juniper remained forever green.

43

# A PERILOUS COURTSHIP

Many a tale of enchantment in ages past involved the overcoming of a series of tests, but success could have an unexpected result. As evidence of fate's twisting ways, Chinese storytellers cited a chain of events that began when a peasant woodcutter went into a bamboo forest one morning.

Wandering in the cool green shadows, the man came upon an old woman clad in the white robes of a widow and bent over a chessboard. She looked up at the peasant, more in expectation than surprise, and gestured to the empty seat opposite her.

The man hesitated, wondering aloud what stakes he could offer for the game. Had he no lands, the widow asked, nor jewels, nor jade? He shook his head. She gazed at him for a long moment, then asked if he had any sons. Smiling at last, he answered that indeed he was rich in sons, with three fine boys. The old woman smiled too, saying that she had as many daughters. She proposed that they play three games. For each that the peasant won, she would send a daughter to marry one of his sons. For each game he lost, he must send a son to marry into her household.

Thinking of three fat dowries, the man nodded, and they began. The shadows grew long as game followed game. At dusk, the peasant stood up. He had lost all of the games and all of his sons. The widow rose too, and pointed to a dark valley in the distance. Her home was there, she said, and there she

45

would expect his eldest son in the morning. The second son must arrive three days later and the youngest one three days after him.

At their father's command, each son left for the widow's valley on the appointed day. When the seventh day dawned, the youngest son said farewell to his father and set out to meet his bride. A ragged stranger joined him on the road and asked his destination. As the stranger listened to the story of the widow, her daughters and the brothers who had gone before, his pace grew slower, until at last he stopped and bowed his head. Sorrowfully, he told the youth that the old woman was a witch with just one daughter. She had lured many young men to their deaths, including the stranger's own son many years before. The two brothers were surely dead as well.

In horror the young man turned back toward his father's house, but the stranger stopped him. He said that a beautiful bride awaited her bridegroom and that he must go to her. As he spoke, he handed the boy an iron pearl, an iron rod and the branch of a cherry tree, calling them wedding gifts. They might have saved his own son, he said, had he known of the witch's treachery.

Clutching his three strange gifts, the bridegroom entered the witch's gate. A lion leaped from the shadows and, without thinking, the youth threw the iron pearl at the beast. The lion chased it and, like a great kitten, began to play with it. As the young man ran toward the witch's door, a tiger sprang from the bushes. The youth hurled the iron rod into its jaws. The tiger lay down to gnaw on it, and the bridegroom climbed the steps of the witch's house.

47

Because his hands were trembling too much to knock, he pushed the door open with the cherry branch. As it swung wide, a huge block of iron crashed to the floor, grazing his fingertips and crushing the branch. The youth climbed over it into an empty chamber. With a shout, he announced himself. An old woman's voice floated back from an inner courtyard, calling to him to find his new mother-in-law in the garden. Until he discovered her hiding-place, the wedding could not begin.

When he stepped into the garden, another voice, younger and sweeter, whispered to him from a window. He turned to meet the eyes of a girl lovelier than a lotus newly opened. He was transfixed, and could only listen as she told him that her mother had transformed herself into a peach, half red and half green, hanging among the fruit espaliered on the garden wall. The green side was only her cloak, but if he bit into the red side, his teeth would find her cheek and the pain would restore her true shape.

Ready to prove himself to the beautiful girl, the young man strode to the peach tree. Among its branches, one peach, swollen larger than the rest, glowed red on one side and green on the other. Although the sun shone brightly, the peach felt icy as he picked it and sunk his teeth into the red flesh.

The fruit burst open in his hand and the witch appeared in full-blown fury, her cheek dark with blood. While she hissed and spat at him, the bridegroom boldly demanded that the wedding now take place. The witch grew silent, studying him, then answered slyly that she had no drum to beat at the

ceremony. He must steal the drum of the
monkey-king in the Western Mountains.

The witch vanished and the bridegroom
turned to leave, despairing. Everyone knew
of the monkey-king's palace guard of sharp-
toothed apes. As the youth passed the
daughter's window, she leaned out to him
again. She whispered that if he rolled in the
mud beside the Western Lake, the apes would
mistake him for a kinsman and welcome him.
Then she gave him a needle, some lime and a
pot of oil, saying that he must throw these
behind him if danger threatened.

Crossing the valley to the Western Lake,
the young man waded into the ooze and
rolled until he was caked with mud. The sun
dried his sticky disguise as he climbed to the
mountain palace. A hundred sharp-toothed
faces appeared at the windows, then vanished
as the great gate swung open. The apes
poured through the gateway, calling the
young man Grandfather and lifting him high.

Greeting the apes as sons of his sons, the
bridegroom announced that he was hungry.
At once, they rushed away to order a feast.
The young man found the drum hanging
inside the gate. He pick it up and fled.

In moments, the apes came screaming after
him. When they drew close, he tossed his
bride's needle over his shoulder. Glinting in
the sun, it splintered into a forest of needles
that impaled dozens of the apes. The youth
threw a handful of lime at the others. It grew
into a mountain of acrid powder, burning the
apes who tried to surmount it. Toward his
remaining pursuers he flung the pot of oil,
which bubbled up into an oily mountain too
slippery for them to climb.

When he reached the witch's house again, the bridegroom presented her with the drum and demanded that the wedding take place. The witch praised him for his courage and cleverness, adding sweetly that such a hero must dine properly before his marriage. She presented him with a pair of ivory chopsticks and a red lacquer tray bearing delicacies in fine porcelain bowls: a crystalline soup made from the nests of rare mountain-dwelling songbirds, heaps of candied plums and loquats, glazed meats and sauces artfully combining sweetness and sourness, subtlety and fiery spice. But he had eaten nothing since leaving his father's house, and craved only simply savors. Declining the rich foods on offer, he accepted instead the bowl of fine wheaten noodles she held out to him.

The youth, replete from his meal, was looking about for his bride when suddenly he bent double and gasped in pain. Laughing, the witch vanished. A serving girl rushed to his side and led him to the bride's chamber. At her mistress' bidding, she tied him to a beam by his feet and beat him with his own sandals. One by one, ten writhing snakes fell from his mouth. The bride shuddered. She said they must be wed that night and flee at dawn from her murderous mother.

Surprised to find that the youth still lived, the witch agreed to marry them at once. After the ceremony, the couple retreated to the bridal chamber, where the daughter had hidden a tattered umbrella and a cock. She gave them to her husband, and the pair hurried into the night.

They had walked several miles when the morning stillness was broken by a whirring

53

sound. The wife quickly told her husband to shield himself with the umbrella and throw the cock out into the path ahead, for her mother had sent a knife flying after them. Just as he did so, a blade dropped from the sky, pierced the bird's heart and flew back toward the witch's house.

The wife warned that the danger might not be over yet. If the witch realized that the blade was covered with cock's blood instead of human blood, she would send the knife back. As she spoke, the whirring noise returned. The young man looked to his wife, who told him that the knife must strike her, for she was of a race that could—if magical precautions were taken—live again. She instructed her husband to take her body to his father's house and seal it in a lotus jar. When forty-nine days had passed, she would come to life once more.

Without another word, she stepped from under the umbrella and welcomed the knife to her breast. When it had flown away, her weeping husband gathered her body into his arms and carried her home. He placed her gently in a lotus jar, sealed it and sank to the ground for his long vigil.

Weeks passed while the devoted young husband ate and slept and waited in the shadow of the jar. At dawn on the forty-eighth day, a moan roused him from slumber. He leaped to his feet as another moan echoed from the jar. Afraid to leave her sealed up any longer, he broke the jar. His wife fell into his embrace, opened her eyes and asked him why he had not waited just one more day. Then she closed her eyes in the sleep from which there is no waking.

# Chapter Two

# FORTUNE'S WHEEL

Whether apt or ill-deserved, the good and bad fortunes of humankind were sometimes imposed through happenstance and quirks of fate. Luck, as much as merit, might pave the way to wealth or happiness; coincidence might be the agency of a well-merited reward or punishment.

In the ages when divinities walked the earth, much as lords of the manor paced out the bounds of their feudal fiefs, mortals who crossed the paths of gods could find their lives forever altered. Women and men alike became objects of celestial lust. Those who spurned advances from on high were punished by losing their human shapes, or their very lives. Yet anyone who yielded to an importuning god might discover that the price of divine caresses was vengeful pursuit by that deity's aggrieved spouse. Walking on sacred ground also had its dangers, and ignorance of the boundaries of the precincts was not deemed sufficient defense by a violated divinity.

Other mortals attracted not lust, but superhuman anger. The unwitting rupture of a taboo or slaughter of a sacred beast might bring disaster not only to the miscreants, but to their friends, their kin, their entire nation.

Dame Fortune, as conceived and personified by the ancient poets, had a fine sense of irony. Presiding over her giant wheel, she brought low the mighty and lifted the poor and humble to heights unimagined. Through her ministrations, a life that began in a palace could end in a pigsty, and those who woke wretched in the morning might find themselves gloriously happy by sunset. At any moment, the dial was likely to lurch and turn. Accordingly, persons of high degree were well advised to shun complacency; dwellers in the lower depths could nourish themselves on the hope for better days.

The Fates might be capricious, but they were not to be defied. The old lore pictured them as weavers, threading and knotting the skeins of human life. Bent over their loom, they carried a grim warning for malcontents. Anyone who heard a prophecy and rebelled against it suffered a doom far darker than did simple victims of mischance. Destiny, moving in its solemn march across the ages, brooked no human interventions, and those who railed against its dictates were first mocked and then destroyed.

57

# Parrying the Forces of Fate

In times past, the Gypsies of Transylvania believed that every child at its birth was visited by three strange beings in white. Some said they were the Fates, come to ordain the child's life. Their decrees were irrevocable; all who fought against them were doomed to failure.

One tale, which traveled with the Gypsies to many parts of the world, told of a poor boy destined to know great fortune, and a King who tried many times, but vainly, to alter that destiny.

The boy was a charcoal-burner's son. Into the humble hut on his birthnight the Fates came and gathered around the cradle. The first foretold a grave misfortune. The second granted the means to turn it to good. The third was more specific. The boy would marry the daughter of the King of that country; she had also been born that very night.

By one of those strange coincidences so often wrought by chance, the King overheard the prophecies. Lost after a day's hunting, he had sought shelter in the hut. The moans of the wife in labor had woken him. The whispers of the otherworldly beings quite destroyed his rest. Joy at news of his daughter's birth warred with rage at her future, ignoble marriage.

As early light began to streak the sky, the King heard weeping. The charcoal-burner's wife had died and he mourned the loss of a wife and a mother for his son.

The King seized his chance. With hypocritical words of comfort, he offered to take the boy and have him brought up by his servants. Later he could be given work in the kitchens or stable.

The charcoal-burner agreed to the plan; it was all he could do for his son. After leading the King to the city road, he handed over the wicker basket which was the baby's cradle, touched the child lingeringly on the cheek with his finger, and turned away, bowed down with grief.

The King, without a thought for the helpless infant, threw it and the basket into a fast-flowing stream. Then he hurried to the city, where bells pealed joyously to welcome his newborn daughter.

Twenty years passed and the girl grew into a beautiful woman. The time had come when the King must find a husband for her. So he set out one day to visit a neighboring monarch who had sons of a suitable age. The weather was hot, and the King soon called a halt to the cortege and ordered a servant to water the horses from the stream of a wayside mill. A young man of extraordinary grace came out to offer his help, and the miller, wiping his hands on his apron, was drawn from his work by the lively commotion.

The King congratulated him on his handsome son and the miller was emboldened to tell a strange story. A number of years before, he had dragged a basket from the surging waters of the millrace. Inside he had found that very boy, miraculously preserved. The miller and his wife had adopted the foundling as their own, and he had brought them much joy.

So this was the child the King had aimed to kill. He smiled and nodded as the tale unfolded, but in his heart he was infuriated that his murderous scheme had been thwarted. He must find another way

*Three handmaidens of fate spoke a prophecy over a newborn infant's head, promising this peasant child the King's daughter as a bride. Witnessing the scene by chance, the displeased monarch set out to defy the decree of fate.*

to dispose of an undesirable son-in-law.

Seeming to request with hesitancy where he might have commanded, he asked the the miller's son to take an urgent message back to the Queen. The boy's eyes lit up with excitement at the chance to go inside a palace. Perhaps he would even catch sight of the Princess, famed for her wondrous beauty. But the message the young man carried was a ruthless command to the Queen to have its bearer beheaded without delay or trial.

As he made his way to the city, the youth fell in with a white-clad woman journeying in the same direction. Full of importance, he told her where he was going and showed her the scrolled message, sealed and addressed to the Queen. As they moved on together, his limbs grew strangely heavy, his eyelids longed to close. Finally he could go no farther. He lay down to sleep on a grassy mound.

When he awoke, his companion was gone. He hurried on, eager to deliver his message. Words cannot describe his bewildered joy when the Queen read out

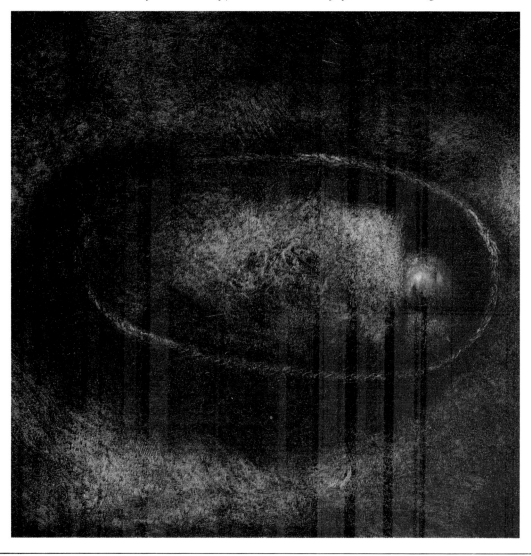

*The King put the infant in a river, expecting that he would drown, but*
*the baby floated downstream into the loving hands of fosterparents,*
*who raised him to manhood.*

the words he had carried. It seemed he had found favor with the King, who saw in him more than a miller's son. He was to be welcomed with all ceremony, attired in silks and velvets, feasted and fêted. He was their daughter's future husband.

The King returned to find the palace humming with wedding preparations. The couple had no sooner met than they loved, so the King was greeted with grateful looks by the young man whose death he desired. And his daughter threw her arms joyously around him, vowing she could not have chosen better herself.

The King, by now well practiced in deceitful smiles, desired to see again the message which had achieved this happy union; it was well worth keeping for posterity. When he had read the letter ordering marriage instead of murder, yet in his own hand, he questioned the youth closely about his journey. At mention of the chance companion in white, the King realized that he was once again in conflict with the magical forces of fate. He knew without doubt that the white-clad woman was the same mysterious stranger who had foretold the boy's royal marriage on the day of his birth. And it was she who had changed the message.

Desperately the King sought another way to rid himself of the boy. He summoned him. It was of course no matter to him, he claimed, that the lad brought neither wealth nor nobility with him. Yet, before his marriage, would the boy not like to prove to the world that he had valor as well as good looks? A challenge fit for a hero and future King was what he had in mind. He then suggested that the boy might find, and bring back, just three golden hairs of the sun-king.

The youth, overwhelmed with gratitude, dazzled by wealth, overpowered by love, had the courage of twenty men. That the sun-king was a dangerous demigod, with a temper reputedly as hot as his blazing orb, did not worry him.

He went on a long journey. Over high mountains and across rushing rivers he traveled, until he came to a great black lake. An old man in a white boat waited to row him across. When the youth spoke of his mission to the sun-king, the boatman asked a favor. The sun lord saw all, knew all. He would be able to say how the ferryman might free himself from the curse that forced him to ferry passengers forever over the lake.

An uphill journey brought the youth to a walled city. He asked the guard at the gate for directions to the sun-king's palace. If that was his destination, said the guard as he pointed out the way, would he kindly ask the King why the stream that ran through the town, and that magically restored all who bathed in it to youth, had suddenly gone dry?

More days of travel, always upward, brought the boy to a village on a plain. He came to a woman sitting beneath an apple tree. When he asked the way to the sun-king's palace, the woman pointed to distant turrets, high on a crag. She was glad he was going there. She and her neighbors had a question for the sun-king. Why did their precious tree, once the bearer of apples that restored the sick

*Sent on a perilous mission to steal three hairs from the sun-king's*
*head, the hero was assisted by the mother of the solar lord,*
*who plucked the strands from her son's head as he slept.*

to health, no longer give them any fruit?

Toward evening the boy reached the palace. He was kindly welcomed by an old woman. He told her why he wanted the golden hairs and the answers to three questions. The woman, the sun-king's mother, said her son would soon be home. Each day he left as a golden-haired boy, returning as a worn old man. She promised the youth the hairs and the answers, but he must hide in a water barrel, lest the sun-king's heat burn him.

Ancient but commanding, the sun-king entered the palace. His mother fussed about him, urging him to eat, as all mothers do. Then he rested his head on her lap and fell into a profound slumber.

When she felt his head grow heavy, she deftly plucked a single hair. The sun-king awoke with a start, asking what was amiss. His mother told of the villagers and their barren apple tree. What, she wondered, prevented the tree from bearing fruit? The King said that a serpent was gnawing at its roots. Only kill that, he said, and the tree would be fruitful once more. Then he fell asleep again.

When she roused him by plucking a second hair, she spoke of the dried-up stream. The King said that the citizens must kill the toad blocking its course, and the waters would flow again.

Awoken yet again by the removal of the third hair, the King heard of the ferryman. Let him, he said, hand his oars to his next passenger and leap from the boat as it reached land. The spell would thus be transferred to a new boatman, and the old man would be free to die.

In the morning, after the sun-king's departure, the woman gave the boy three long golden hairs and told him the answers to his questions. He kissed her farewell and thanked her profoundly.

When the villagers, at his behest, slew the serpent, they found the apple tree's powers restored. The townsfolk swiftly killed the toad that had dammed their stream. At the black lake, the boy waited until he was safely ashore before he told the boatman how to escape.

When the youth returned, safe and triumphant, with the golden hairs, the King failed altogether to muster a smile, but the rapture of the Princess's greeting was compensation enough. After the first flurry of arrival, the youth began to tell his tale. The King, though brooding and absorbed by dark thoughts, was struck by the mention of apples of health and waters of youth. Those, to a man of middle years, were worth more than golden hairs, and he must get them for himself.

Unaccompanied, he galloped full tilt toward the somber lake, and summoned the boatman to row him across. The white boat had not quite reached the opposite side when, under one pretext or another, the old man persuaded the King to take the oars. Then, nimbly in spite of his age, the ferryman leaped ashore.

For the King there was no escape. He was left, spellbound, to row the boat to eternity—time enough to reflect on the implacability of fate. The charcoal-burner's son married his Princess, as it had been ordained from birth that he would.

As a punishment for seeking to defy destiny, the old King was tricked into perpetual servitude as a ferryman on an enchanted lake.

# Beloved of the Gods

In the dangerous days when supernatural beings walked the earth, mortal women cast wary eyes toward amorous strangers, who might reveal themselves as demons, fairies or even gods. With their own powers of enchantment limited to beauty, wit and virtue, these humans wisely feared the attentions of suitors whose passions and jealousies were armed with magic. They were well warned of these perils in songs and stories that spread from the heights of the Balkans to Iceland's bleak shores.

One legend told of a maiden named Florilor, who tended her flocks in the mountain pastures of Rumania. During the precious weeks of alpine summer, Florilor took her sheep to the highest meadow, closest to the sun. Loosing her hair, she lay back among the mountain blossoms and turned her face to the sky.

Each day, the sun's rays shone longer and more warmly on Florilor. One afternoon, basking sleepily in the meadow, she grew uncomfortably hot. The sunlight seemed to burn through her closed eyelids, and she buried her face in the tall grass. At last, longing for shade, she rose. Before her stood the sun-god himself, his brilliant aspect fiery with desire. Noticing her perfect beauty from the heavens, he had lingered above her meadow each noon. This day, he would claim her. He held out one shining hand in a gesture that was both invitation and command.

Shielding her eyes, she turned away from him. Even more than she feared the white heat of his touch, Florilor feared the chill of the coming dusk, when the passion-spent god would surely leave her,

ruined and alone. Kneeling among the flowers, she shook her head in refusal.

Too proud to ask again, the god disdained to take the girl by force. Instead, with a single word he punished her insolent wilfulness, transforming her into a chicory plant where she knelt. Ever after, the chicory turned its many-rayed flowers to follow the sun's path across the sky, humbly folding its petals at dusk.

Immortal maidens, too, risked the wrath of more powerful beings whose desires and jealousies they roused. Generations of bards wandering in the rain-washed half-light of Ireland sang of Etain, a fairy who dwelled on the cliffs of the western coast. A Celtic poet's description of Etain preserved her beauty for all time: "Her eyes were blue as hyacinth, her lips as red as Parthian leather. High, smooth, soft and white were her shoulders, clear white her long fingers. White as the foam of a wave was her side, long and slender, yielding, smooth, soft as wool. The radiance of love was in her eyes, the flush of pleasure on her cheeks."

Etain's only mirror was a rocky pool in the cliffs. One day, as she sat beside it combing her golden hair, a face appeared beside hers in the water's trembling surface. The stranger was Midhir the Proud, son of the fairies' god-king Dagda. In a voice as sweet as song, filled with all the enchantment of his race, the Prince wooed the fairy maiden. As she swayed to the music and magic of his words, Midhir took her in his arms. The next morning she rode behind his saddle to Bri

Leith, his home in the north country.

When Midhir's retinue came out to greet him on the steps of Bri Leith, Etain saw at their head a richly robed woman whose possessive gaze took in the palace, the servants and Midhir himself. The girl understood at once that the woman was the wife of Midhir and that she herself arrived not as a bride but as a rival.

Midhir's wife was Fuamnach, a Fairy Princess powerful not only as chatelaine of Bri Leith but as an artful sorceress. She was cold with rage as she watched Midhir hand the girl gently down from his horse. The Prince approached his wife with an easy laugh, dismissive of her anger and his own transgression. Yet his laughter died as he saw her raise her magical rod. With a blow swifter than her husband's staying hand, she struck Etain across the face.

Instantly, the girl began to lose her shape and substance, melting into a pool of water at Fuamnach's feet. But even as the sorceress stood triumphantly over the pool, its outline wavered and changed. It became a serpent, hissing reproachfully at Fuamnach, then dissolved into a butterfly that rose, unsteadily at first, into the air and flew away. Fuamnach, who had not reckoned on Etain's immortality, stared after the iridescent creature, wings glittering in the uncertain sunlight, then took her place at Midhir's side.

Afraid to challenge his wife's potent magic, Midhir mourned his beautiful Etain for many days until, borne on a morning breeze, the butterfly reappeared. It fluttered around the Prince, spreading a sweet fragrance and a musical charm in the air. Midhir knew that this fragile creature, too delicate to touch, was all that now remained of Etain.

The butterfly haunted Midhir's steps day and night. Fuamnach soon wearied of this reminder of her husband's infidelity always hovering just beyond the reach of her magical rod. At last, calling on all her darkest powers, she summoned a tempest whose bitter wind snatched up the butterfly and tossed it high into the air. The creature was buffeted far over the hills and forests to the harsh cliffe of Etain's homeland. There, the wind dropped and the butterfly fell to the earth.

It crawled among the chill rocks, wet with salt spray. When it tried to fly, the wind dashed it back upon the rocks, its powdery wings tattered and soaked.

A prisoner of sea and storm, the butterfly suffered for seven years until another Fairy Prince, Midhir's half-brother Oengus, wandered along the cliffe. Noticing the glimmer of bright wings among the rocks, he gathered the battered creature in his hands and carried it away. At home, he stocked a bower with fragrant blossoms for the butterfly. On his travels, he carried it with him in a crystal cage. With eyes that could see past the present plain as daylight, he perceived this was no ordinary winged insect. His thoughts touched Etain's. He discovered that the rainbow-colored wings concealed a human spirit.

Oengus tried all the hidden arts at his command to free her from her captivity.

*When the Irish fairy-lord Midhir the Proud fell in love with a beautiful maiden, his jealous wife turned her rival into a butterfly. Buffeted by storms, the creature alighted on a goblet's rim and was accidentally swallowed.*

For weeks he uttered spells, concocted charms, combed the woods and meadows for the rare and potent herbs that were part of the fairy race's pharmacopoeia.

These efforts were partially successful: He was able to restore Etain to her natural shape each night, and slept in her arms, but the metamorphosis only lasted for a few hours at a time. At dawn her body would shrink, her features disappear and her form become that of a butterfly once more. Fuamnach's sorcery—forged of jealousy and a wronged wife's injured pride—was stronger than any powers that Oengus could command.

Try as Oengus might to keep this secret, the servants of his house were sharp-eyed and the walls were thin. Tongues wagged in the kitchen and scullery, rumors were served up along with the bread and cheese to the grooms and stableboys, and before long the story of Oengus and his strange paramour traveled down the rutted lanes, into the alehouses and horse fairs, and far beyond the Prince's own domains.

Tales of the exquisite butterfly spread across Ireland. When news reached Bri Leith, Fuamnach knew at once that her rival was free. She invited Oengus to visit Bri Leith. When he arrived, her greetings were effusive. She offered him the best room in her house to lodge in, and insisted on overseeing the servants who carried in his chests and bundles, to be sure that everything was arranged for his greatest comfort. Then she ordered up a feast, of many rare dishes and delicacies, to refresh him after his journey.

While he was occupied in the enjoyment of a roasted boar and the sampling of the finest wines her cellars afforded, Fuamnach excused herself for a moment and left the hall. She stole into his bedchamber. Slipping the catch of the crystal cage, she tempted the butterfly into the air. As it fluttered above her, the sorceress called up another wind which carried the creature away.

The butterfly was tossed helplessly over the countryside until at last a final gust dashed it against the roof of a great fortress in Ulster, the home of a mortal man named Etar. It fell through the gaping chimney hole over the smoky hearth of the dining hall. Spiraling down into the gloom, the creature dropped straight into the cup of Etar's wife as she drank. With a noisy gulk, the woman swallowed the butterfly with her wine.

Although greed had already fattened her, Etar's wife grew even rounder in the passing weeks. When nine months had gone by, she gave birth to a baby girl of remarkable beauty. When asked what she would name her daughter, the woman answered, "Etain," though it was a name she had not known before.

The child grew, fulfilling all the promise of her early beauty. When Eochy, High King of the Irish, went searching for his kingdom's loveliest maiden to wed, he traveled no farther than the fortress of Etar. Clad in fine gossamer robes that shimmered with all the colors of a butterfly's wing, Etain married the High King and ruled with him as Qeeen of all the land.

# The Warrior King who Scorned a Goddess

Many thousands of years ago, in the epoch of the Great Flood which nearly wiped out humankind, there lived in Mesopotamia a warrior called Gilgamesh, King of Uruk, whose majesty, strength and deeds of astounding courage were never eclipsed in the whole history of heroes. Yet, through his pride, he humiliated a powerful goddess and so blighted his life.

Gilgamesh was born to the world fully grown, two parts god and one part man. His mother was a goddess, from whom he inherited tremendous strength and unearthly beauty; from his father, a priest, he inherited mortality. Suspended thus between divine and human life—framed like a god but doomed to die like a human—Gilgamesh was racked by an insatiable restlessness, an urgent need to gain a kind of immortality through a career of unparalleled heroism.

The energy for this ambition knew no limits. It drove Gilgamesh from combat to combat without letting him rest. When he rested, his mind was tormented with dreams of dying.

Their King's lust for glory exhausted and terrified the people of Uruk. When he could find no enemies to contend with, Gilgamesh fought the sons of his own city. Granted every comfort by their ruler except safety, the people begged the gods to save them. Hearing them, the gods sent Enkidu to divert his attention and deflect his energies.

Though it was not possible to make a man braver and more fierce than Gilgamesh, Enkidu was a match for him: tall, handsome and strong as a star. The gods set him down in the wilderness and drew the Lord of Uruk to meet him, unarmed. The two heroes wrestled like giants for many days, splitting open the very earth with their roars. When Gilgamesh finally threw Enkidu to the ground, he looked at him and loved him like a brother.

From that day on, the King showered Enkidu with riches and sat him on his left hand for all the rulers of the world to bow down before; Enkidu served his conqueror with a loyalty fueled by the purest devotion. Together the two friends journeyed in quest of adventure in the wild places of the earth. Together they dared to enter the Great Forest of Cedars, where Gilgamesh slew the monstrous guardian, a thunder-voiced giant called Khumbaba, by summoning all the elements—earth, air, water and fire—to his aid. It was through this last victory that Gilgamesh excited the lust of the goddess who would one day bring him low.

Begrimed with traveling and soaked with Khumbaba's blood, Gilgamesh was weary; but his heart sang with the glory he had won. Laughing, he threw off his tattered clothes and bathed. Then he dressed in magnificent robes and put on the crown of Uruk. He had thought himself alone, but his every movement had been carefully watched by Ishtar, the goddess of love, hiding unseen. At the sight of the mighty warrior naked, her blood had raced. Seeing him dressed again so splendidly, she could contain her desire no longer. Running after Gilgamesh, she caught him by the sleeve and commanded

*Half divine and half human, the Mesopotamian hero Gilgamesh excited the amorous interest of Ishtar, goddess of love and war. But when he resisted all her blandishments, her anger was aroused as well.*

# A slanderer undone

The unwanted attentions of lustful mortals could be just as dangerous as the amorous longings of the gods. So it happened that in ancient Palestine a woman named Zillah suffered at the hands of Hammel, her lecherous neighbor.

Hammel was a merchant, rich enough to purchase anything he desired. On land, his caravans flowed ceaselessly along the desert trade routes of Africa and Asia, ferrying wheat and amber, precious metals, silks and spices. At sea, his fleet of cargo ships dominated western commerce, taking tin from the blue-painted Britons, bringing slaves to the marts of Athens and Alexandria. But all his revenues and profits could not entice Zillah to his bed.

Honeyed persuasions and veiled threats were equally fruitless. Losing patience, Hammel warned that if Zillah rejected him once more, he would accuse her publicly of prostitution and licentious acts.

This was no empty threat. In that stern country, such crimes were punishable by death, and a man's word weighed more than a woman's. Yet Zillah spurned him once again. Hammel denounced her to the authorities and her denials counted for nothing. Zillah was condemned to be burned at the stake in the marketplace, in her accuser's presence.

It is written that when the wood was ignited, a great tongue of flame flashed out and consumed Hammel where he stood, and the glowing coals at Zillah's feet turned to roses. Some chroniclers proposed that this was the work of a guardian spirit, coming to the aid of an injured innocent. But others claimed that Zillah's own anger at the outrage drew forth the fire out of heaven and struck her false accuser down.

him to marry her—promising in return the full bounty of heaven's luxuries.

Ishtar's power was great: She was also goddess of war. But Gilgamesh said he would not marry her—would not even be her lover. Lifting her hand from his arm, he recounted a catalog of mortal lovers she had taken in the past and callously disposed of when she had tired of them. He would have none of it. And, in any case, all his affections were centered on Enkidu. Bowing low, the King took his leave and walked on.

Ishtar was too shaken by rage to speak. Never had she been refused in anything. At once she sped to the court of Anu, father of the gods, and fell at his feet. She begged him through her tears to summon for her the Bull of Heaven—a beast so lethal and terrifying that it was kept tethered outside Creation—and send it to gore Gilgamesh to death. Anu hesitated, knowing full well that Gilgamesh had spoken the truth: Ishtar was indeed a fickle and treacherous goddess. As he vacillated, Ishtar screamed: If the bull were not unleashed and sent to earth, she would smash down the doors of hell and bring up the dead to eat food with the living. Anu at once relented.

The bull thundered down to the mortal world. It stamped its massive hooves and a hundred men fell dead; it bellowed out its challenge and blasted two hundred more to shreds. Gilgamesh and Enkidu swiftly armed themselves and went to face the brute. Spying its chosen victim, the bull snorted in derision, smashing the two heroes against the walls of Uruk. But Enkidu, quickly recovering his senses,

vaulted onto the bull's back and grabbed its horns; the beast foamed and thrashed but could not shake him. Seizing his chance, Gilgamesh took hold of the bull's tail and ran the animal through with his spear. It slumped to the ground with a deafening crash, and Gilgamesh cut out its heart.

**m**ortals and immortals were similarly amazed that the hero had again cheated death; but Ishtar was furious. She stalked invisibly across the rooftops of Uruk, crying out curses on the head of Gilgamesh. Hearing the goddess, Enkidu ripped the skin from the bull and flung the bloody hide in the direction of her voice, shouting he would do the same to her if he could get his hands on her, and would wrap her in her own entrails for good measure. The people marveled at Enkidu's audacity and proclaimed Gilgamesh the noblest of heroes.

Ishtar meditated on her revenge: How much more insult and sacrilege must she endure from this arrogant King and his filthy catamite—for the sake of whom she had been rejected? Then she saw how she could torture Gilgamesh to death with grief: She began to poison Enkidu through his dreams.

At first, the nightmares that stormed Enkidu's sleeping brain were filled with pictures of the gods in council, passing judgment against him for helping Gilgamesh kill the Bull of Heaven. He awoke, terrified that he was under sentence of death. Gilgamesh reassured his friend and calmed him back to sleep. But the evil

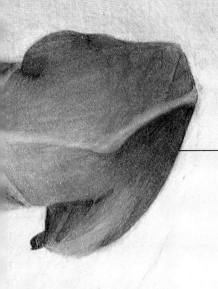

*Ishtar dispatched the Bull of Heaven to punish Gilgamesh
for his indifference. But the intended victim and his friend Enkidu slew the
monster and flung its hide skyward as a gesture of contempt.*

gnawed into Enkidu's soul, and, convinced that he was condemned to die, he became paralyzed by a delirious sickness. He lay on his bed, floundering from sleep to wakefulness and back again: Everywhere his fevered mind turned, he found death waiting for him.

Powerless to protect him, Gilgamesh sat by the sickbed without moving. Enkidu wept so long and hard for his appalling fate that on the third day he wept his eyes completely away, then lay writhing in the utter dark of blindness. On the tenth day Enkidu was suddenly lucid: He reached out for the King's hand. In the voice of those who embrace death even as they speak, he said that the gods had finally hacked apart the truest ever friendship: Enkidu had now to die.

Gilgamesh rose slowly, walked out onto the steps of the palace and faced the waiting crowds. His face was altered like that of one who had made a long journey. Shattered by sorrow, he told them of the love he had borne Enkidu—the only man he could truly call his brother. With these words he returned to the bedside and felt Enkidu's heart: It was quite still, and the flesh had already begun to stiffen. Piece by piece the King tore off the sumptuous robes that had so aroused Ishtar, and, like a mothering animal robbed of her young, mighty Gilgamesh cowered at Enkidu's feet and cried until the dawn. Then, while the city slept, he dressed in a lion's skin, stole out of Uruk and retreated for a time of mourning into the wilderness whence Enkidu came, taking with him a sorrow that nothing could ever lift.

*Failing to injure Gilgamesh by other means, the goddess sent an illness that killed his beloved comrade, Enkidu. She had her savage satisfaction, for the loss blighted Gilgamesh's life forever.*

# The Wrath of Artemis

Of all the goddesses that were known to the ancients, few were so devoutly worshipped and rightly feared as Artemis, daughter of Zeus and sister of Apollo. She was armed from birth with far-reaching but contradictory powers: She was protectress of all wild things, especially their young, yet she was also patroness of hunting and loved nothing so much as the grueling chase of boar or stag across a mountainside. She was guardian of chastity and healer of the sick; women in labor called out to her to grant them a painless birth. Yet she would not hesitate to spread lingering death among those mortals who displeased her. Exactly what actions would provoke such ugly retribution from the goddess, people were never able to tell, and they spoke of her therefore with the greatest respect, though in their hearts they feared her legendary and violent caprices.

But Artemis was not capricious: She knew her own mind and acted according to considered decisions. She had escaped much of the gods' shameful infighting and petty bickering by choosing to stay apart from them, in the forested mountains of the earth, attended only by her nymphs and chosen animals. Living in this way she had won a measure of independence and a sense of true ownership of territory afforded to few other gods. Only when this propriety was—however inadvertently—interfered with, would Artemis lash out.

One victim of her self-protection was Prince Actaeon, son of Cadmus, whose blundering but innocent trespass earned him an especially grisly death. Actaeon, too, loved the hunt. He rode whenever possible in the mountains, where the ground was most challenging and the game plentiful. One day, when the heat of noon had shortened the shadows and baked dry the blood of the many beasts he had run down and slain, Actaeon called together his weary retainers, congratulated them on their success and told them to prepare to bear the trophies home.

While his servants attended to their tasks, Actaeon dismounted and wandered into the forest, until he came to a place called Gargaphie. He did not know it, but he had stumbled upon Artemis' favorite and most secret haunt. It was a valley, thickly mantled with pine and cypress trees; hidden in its depths, in an oasis of grass, was a shallow cave, naturally vaulted inside with exquisite rocks and overlooking a sparkling pool. When Actaeon emerged from the trees, he was amazed to see a group of naked and beautiful girls laughing and splashing in the water.

At the sight of him they shrieked and tried to cover themselves. Actaeon smiled foolishly with embarrassment and turned to go, but was stopped in his tracks by the voice of a woman, quavering with rage. For the bathers were not mortals, but nymphs who ministered to Artemis—and among them in the water was the goddess herself.

Thinking Actaeon had surprised her deliberately in order to see her naked, Artemis splashed his face from the pool she stood in, and at once antlers erupted out of his head. Terrified, he fled away, feeling his body twist and wrench itself into strange new shapes. He ran faster than ever before and soon reached the grove where the hunting party awaited him. He cried out, but only a tortured bellow came forth. The men looked up and saw before them a mighty stag a prize for any hunter. They grabbed their weapons at once, loosed the hounds and gave chase to their transformed lord. Actaeon reared on his hind legs and bolted. But the wretched Prince had trained his dogs too well: Though he jumped the highest thickets and forded the fullest streams, the tireless killers caught him and ripped out his throat and heart even as he struggled to run. Such was the terrible punishment of Actaeon.

In the same way, Artemis did not shrink from causing monstrous upset in human affairs if her own were marginally infringed. Veterans of Agamemnon's bloody campaign against Troy told how the goddess almost cost their general the war. It happened that, long before Helen was abducted and the great war began, Agamemnon hunted and killed a stag, not knowing that the particular animal was a special favorite of Artemis. The goddess stayed her revenge until Agamemnon was appointed commander of the Greek expeditionary force and had assembled a thousand ships at Aulis, ready to sail.

Then she struck: She stilled the winds to maroon the armada in its port, and then she sowed plague among the soldiers cramped in the bowels of the ships. Realizing the coincidence of these disasters was no natural accident, Agamemnon summoned the seer, Calchas, and de-manded an explanation and a solution. Calchas, sensing the will of Artemis, sadly told Agamemnon of his past misdeed and of the only recompense the aggrieved goddess would accept: the ritual sacrifice of the general's beloved daughter, Iphigenia. Agamemnon was appalled, but he understood that the only way to uphold his honor and serve his cause was to yield his daughter to Artemis' revenge.

Accordingly, he summoned Iphigenia to tell her so; but when she came to him and kissed his hand, he found only lies on his tongue. He told her he had decided she should be married to Achilles, the most famous and handsome of the Greek officers. Iphigenia laughed for joy and clapped her hands. Guilt turned in her father's heart like a knife.

Iphigenia was quickly garlanded and led to the altar, where she stood, radiant, believing she was waiting for her future husband. The priests, meanwhile, waited for Agamemnon to give them the signal to kill her. Behind his daughter's back, Agamemnon wept on his knees. Then, pulling himself to his feet, he nodded to the priests, who swiftly took hold of Iphigenia and drew their knives.

At that very instant, Artemis, seeing Agamemnon's soul flooded with remorse, snatched the girl away, leaving a white hind in her place to receive the blades and spill its blood. Then Artemis breathed life into the winds again, quenched the plague and let Agamemnon sail. Iphigenia she kept, making her a high priestess of her temple.

*To punish the Greek general Agamemnon for inadvertently killing a sacred stag, the goddess Artemis sent a plague that decimated his forces, and stilled the winds to keep his warships in port.*

# The Cruel Reply to a Mortal's Boast

In the grim catalog of divine punishments sustained by erring mortals, none were so cruel as those inflicted on men and women who threatened the ascendancy of the gods. One such offender was the Grecian Queen, Niobe—who wounded the vanity of a goddess and incurred the bitterest revenge, which embraced many wholly innocent of her crime.

Niobe had much to be proud of: Tall and beautiful, she was the daughter of Tantalus, once the most intimate friend of Zeus himself. With her noble husband Amphion, she built and ruled the great city of Thebes; her name was sung by poets everywhere. Yet what most swelled Niobe's heart when she reflected on her life was her motherhood of seven sons and seven daughters. Happiest of all mothers, Niobe once proclaimed the fact for all to hear, and so damned both herself and the very children she adored.

Every year the people of Thebes held a festival to worship Leto, once the mistress of Zeus and the mother of Artemis and Apollo. On this sacred day, scalding pride goaded Niobe to issue an awful challenge: She strode up to the sacrificial altar, swept aside the priests and harangued the startled crowd. Why, she raged, did they make groveling obeisance to a minor goddess whom they only pretended to have seen? Who was she, this jade banished from Zeus's bed with a paltry two children to show for her illicit passion? Why did they not honor Niobe, a properly married matron and mother of the most wonderful children on earth or in heaven—was she not more tangible proof of the glory of motherhood?

The citizens of Thebes, secretly appalled by the Queen's outburst, mumbled and slid away to finish the rites as best they could in their own homes, hoping to appease Leto. But Leto was not appeased. With her children, she had watched the whole episode, aghast at Niobe's sacrilege. There was no need for debate. At Leto's silent bidding, the young deities shrouded themselves in cloud and sped to do vengeance for their slighted mother. They flew to a pavilion outside the city, where Niobe's sons, ignorant of her tirade, were practicing at arms together, running and laughing. Poised overhead, Apollo and Artemis drew their bows, and—one by one—murdered all seven bewildered boys, riddling them with arrows.

News of the slaughter raced to the palace. Amphion, broken with grief, cut his throat; Niobe gathered her daughters and rode to the scene of slaughter. At the sight of the carnage, the girls dropped weeping on the twisted corpses of their brothers. Waiting invisibly, the killers struck once more. Six screaming girls fell dead; the seventh, thinking she was spared, fled to her mother's breast where Artemis, with great deliberation, slew her. Throughout all, Niobe uttered not a sound: Horror had turned her to cold stone. Suddenly, a mighty whirlwind tore over the plain, drew up the rock that had been Niobe and carried her to the summit of distant Mount Sipylus. There, the poets said, she sat evermore, wasting away in the wind and rain, weeping for her folly and her lost children.

# Following the Trail of Corruption

Sometimes fortune's wheel spun without any apparent divine intervention. From ancient India came the tale of a boy who triumphed by making good use of an inherited talisman, at the expense of an unworthy ruler who richly deserved his fall.

The boy's origins were mysterious. It was said that although his father was of the highest caste, his mother was a strange creature, half woman and half spirit, who raised her child in an unpeopled wilderness. Finally, hungering for the society of humankind, the boy decided to desert his lonely homeland for Benares, India's holiest city.

With him he brought a smooth stone of magical potency, his grieving mother's parting gift. Used according to a set of secret instructions, this talisman enabled him to see the footsteps left by men and women long after they had walked over a spot, and to identify who had made them.

He entered Benares, a busy metropolis whose untold wealth had been accumulated by generations of rulers from the commerce of the pilgrims who thronged its holy places. The riches in the city's vaults were at that time in the hands of an undistinguished and miserly King, whose treasure was his sole preoccupation.

The boy's first action was to go to the palace and ask to see the Grand Vizier. He told the minister of the special skill conferred by his magic talisman and offered to place it at the disposal of the King. As he pointed out, he would be able to track down any possible robber and recover stolen treasure. The King jumped at the chance to enlist the boy and, after some haggling, agreed to pay him a daily fee for his services.

For some months the arrangement appeared satisfactory. As the boy's special powers were common knowledge, no robbers risked an attempt on the treasury. The boy simply collected his salary and led a peaceful life in the comfort of the palace, sitting on a rug by the marble fountain, playing chess. Soon, however, the King began to grudge the money the boy was paid for his as yet unproven abilities. He summoned the Vizier and confided his suspicions that the boy might be a fraud who had hit upon an easy way to live in luxury. The King proposed that they should test the boy's claims by staging a robbery themselves.

So, the King and his minister entered the treasury under cover of dark and chose, from the fabulous objects heaped there, many of the finest jewels as well as quantities of coin, all of which they stowed in bags. Heaving the sacks onto their backs, they set off by a circuitous route to find a foolproof hiding-place.

In their soft slippers they trod three times round the palace, passing without apparent trace over the clean cool marble of the terraces, then along the neat paths that wound through the scented gardens. They climbed a wall with the aid of a ladder, dragging the sacks over with them, and came at last to a stone-built pool set in a lawn. Here they dropped the sacks into the water. When the booty had sunk out of sight they returned, undetected.

The next morning the King raised the alarm. The boy immediately applied

*In the old city of Benares, a boy offered his services as thief-catcher to the rich but miserly King. The youth possessed a magic talisman that enabled him to see footsteps on the ground, and to know who made them.*

To test their servant's mettle,
the monarch and his Vizier burgled their own
treasury, and left an intricate trail of
invisible footsteps for the boy to find.

87

himself to his task. From the audience chamber where the King had summoned him, he went straight to the treasure vaults. Then, accompanied in silence by the King and the Vizier, and followed at a distance by a crowd of fascinated courtiers, he walked three times round the palace, threaded his way unhesitatingly through the gardens, sent for a ladder to climb the wall at a particular point, crossed the lawn and stopped at the edge of the pool. There he asked for a diver to be summoned, to bring up from under the water whatever he might find there.

As they waited the boy considered the situation. While following the two sets of footsteps that lay plainly before his eyes, his talisman revealed that they corresponded all too clearly with the feet of the two robed figures walking silently by his side. He kept his perplexity to himself and simply reported that he could see the footsteps of two men, and that they were "men of distinction."

When the diver produced the bags of treasure from the pool, there was a delighted uproar from the onlookers. The boy noticed that the King, however, displayed none of the expected jubilance. After a hastily whispered conference with his Vizier, he allowed his ill-judged suspicions and resentment to lead him even further into trouble; he demanded that the boy should now identify the thieves.

Fearing the consequences, the boy tried to turn aside the King's demand by reminding him that the recovery of the treasure was the most important thing.

But the ruler insisted that the boy should name the criminals. Unbeknown to his subjects, he and his Vizier had for a long time been purloining gold from the public exchequer to fill their own yawning purses. He needed to ascertain if the boy's powers of detection posed a real threat.

Still anxious to avoid the crisis that a revelation would bring, the boy made a direct appeal to the King to be cautious, bidding him think what the people would do if a man whom they trusted and relied upon was proved to be a thief and a liar. The King—apparently unable to heed even an open warning—laughed, and replied that unless the boy named the culprits he would be driven from the palace.

At last the boy stated simply that the King and the Vizier were the thieves. At first the crowd greeted this news with incredulity. Then they began to murmur among themselves about their ruler's ignoble deceit. One question led to another: Where had the taxes gone that had been earmarked to build a hostel for poor pilgrims? Why was the King's treasury so full of jewels and costly ornaments when the granaries were almost empty? How had the Vizier managed to build himself a palace in the country that was almost as grand as the King's in town?

With so many pairs of reproachful eyes upon them, the two scoundrels knew that more than their footsteps had been exposed. The King who had so betrayed his position was forced to abdicate and go into dishonorable exile with his Vizier, while the boy received the homage of the multitude and, in due course, became King in his place.

## A well-intentioned blunder

An old Chinese tale recalled the beginning of time, when the Heavenly Emperor ruled from his throne among the stars and people labored endlessly in the fields on earth. As he looked down, the Heavenly Emperor was saddened by how hard his subjects worked and how terribly hungry they were. So he resolved to provide them with enough to eat.

He determined that food once every three days should be sufficient. Happy with his magnanimity, he called upon one of his minions, the Star Ox, to go down to announce the new order.

How the Star Ox got down to earth, or what the men and women who saw the celestial beast's arrival thought of it, is not recorded. Nor is there any record of the feelings of the starving people when the splendid ox made his announcement. What was passed down was the Heavenly Emperor's reaction to the ox's words. The ox had garbled the message in the telling, promising three meals each day instead of one meal every three days. The Emperor was furious. His proclamations, whether delivered by a stupid underling or by his own august self, were as immutable as stone, as inevitable as the monsoon.

Although there was no way that people could produce enough food to fill their cooking pots and ceramic bowls three times a day, the Heavenly Emperor was bound by his word, as it was spoken by his messenger. Since the ox had made the error, the Heavenly Emperor decreed that he would have to correct it throughout eternity by living on earth and plowing the soil.

It was not the ox's fault that he had gotten the message wrong. But it was the law of heaven that the Emperor had to provide what had been promised in his name. And the necessity of keeping strictly to the order of things redounded to the benefit of all humankind.

# Wanderers on a Road without End

Throughout all the old kingdoms of Europe and Asia Minor, ordinary folk whispered of their eerie encounters with a man who walked the earth as punishment for a terrible crime. The peace of death was forever denied him; so, too, the solace of oblivion. This wanderer had many different names and guises, and the tales told about him were as numberless as the footsteps of his journey.

Some accounts painted him as a vagabond, with a pack on his back. He might be found jostling among the polyglot crowds of a busy metropolis, brooding on lonely mountainsides, standing at a crossroads where suicides were buried, or slowly picking his way across rubble-strewn beaches, where the bones of fallen sea birds lay bleaching in the sun.

Poets and sages could not agree if all the sightings recorded, from the Caucasus to the cloudy coast of Flanders, were of the same miserable sinner. Some speculated that there were a number of these wretched wraiths crossing the world, oblivious to one another as they paced out the measure of eternity. Each one expiated a different crime, or fled a different Nemesis. The earliest of all known fugitives was a man who slew his own brother at the beginning of time. The Hebrew chroniclers called

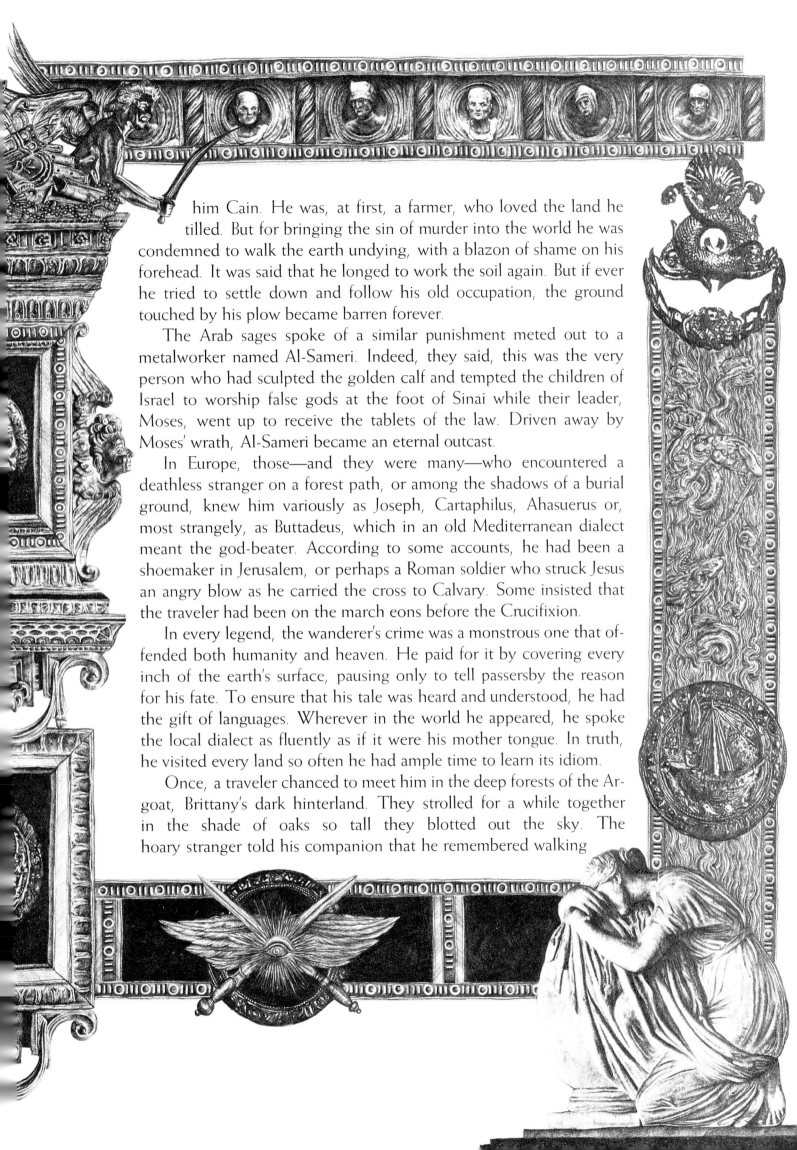

him Cain. He was, at first, a farmer, who loved the land he tilled. But for bringing the sin of murder into the world he was condemned to walk the earth undying, with a blazon of shame on his forehead. It was said that he longed to work the soil again. But if ever he tried to settle down and follow his old occupation, the ground touched by his plow became barren forever.

The Arab sages spoke of a similar punishment meted out to a metalworker named Al-Sameri. Indeed, they said, this was the very person who had sculpted the golden calf and tempted the children of Israel to worship false gods at the foot of Sinai while their leader, Moses, went up to receive the tablets of the law. Driven away by Moses' wrath, Al-Sameri became an eternal outcast.

In Europe, those—and they were many—who encountered a deathless stranger on a forest path, or among the shadows of a burial ground, knew him variously as Joseph, Cartaphilus, Ahasuerus or, most strangely, as Buttadeus, which in an old Mediterranean dialect meant the god-beater. According to some accounts, he had been a shoemaker in Jerusalem, or perhaps a Roman soldier who struck Jesus an angry blow as he carried the cross to Calvary. Some insisted that the traveler had been on the march eons before the Crucifixion.

In every legend, the wanderer's crime was a monstrous one that offended both humanity and heaven. He paid for it by covering every inch of the earth's surface, pausing only to tell passersby the reason for his fate. To ensure that his tale was heard and understood, he had the gift of languages. Wherever in the world he appeared, he spoke the local dialect as fluently as if it were his mother tongue. In truth, he visited every land so often he had ample time to learn its idiom.

Once, a traveler chanced to meet him in the deep forests of the Argoat, Brittany's dark hinterland. They strolled for a while together in the shade of oaks so tall they blotted out the sky. The hoary stranger told his companion that he remembered walking

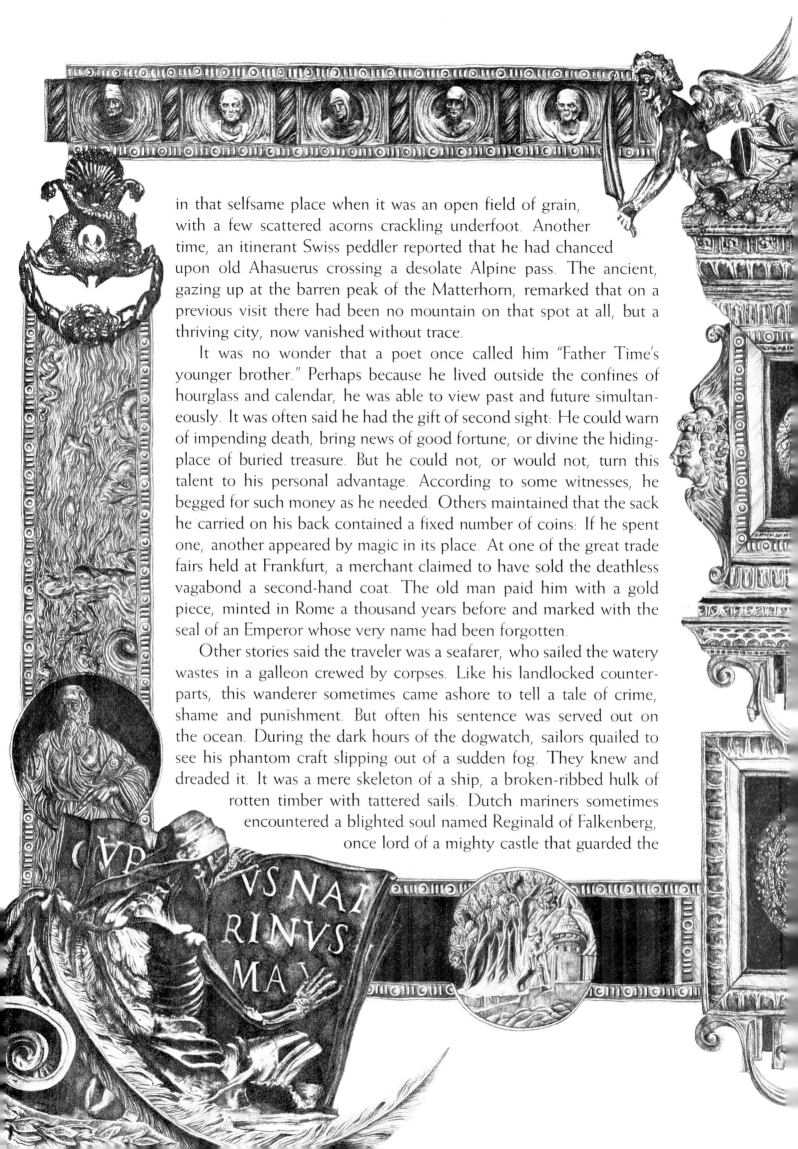

in that selfsame place when it was an open field of grain, with a few scattered acorns crackling underfoot. Another time, an itinerant Swiss peddler reported that he had chanced upon old Ahasuerus crossing a desolate Alpine pass. The ancient, gazing up at the barren peak of the Matterhorn, remarked that on a previous visit there had been no mountain on that spot at all, but a thriving city, now vanished without trace.

It was no wonder that a poet once called him "Father Time's younger brother." Perhaps because he lived outside the confines of hourglass and calendar, he was able to view past and future simultaneously. It was often said he had the gift of second sight: He could warn of impending death, bring news of good fortune, or divine the hiding-place of buried treasure. But he could not, or would not, turn this talent to his personal advantage. According to some witnesses, he begged for such money as he needed. Others maintained that the sack he carried on his back contained a fixed number of coins: If he spent one, another appeared by magic in its place. At one of the great trade fairs held at Frankfurt, a merchant claimed to have sold the deathless vagabond a second-hand coat. The old man paid him with a gold piece, minted in Rome a thousand years before and marked with the seal of an Emperor whose very name had been forgotten.

Other stories said the traveler was a seafarer, who sailed the watery wastes in a galleon crewed by corpses. Like his landlocked counter-parts, this wanderer sometimes came ashore to tell a tale of crime, shame and punishment. But often his sentence was served out on the ocean. During the dark hours of the dogwatch, sailors quailed to see his phantom craft slipping out of a sudden fog. They knew and dreaded it. It was a mere skeleton of a ship, a broken-ribbed hulk of rotten timber with tattered sails. Dutch mariners sometimes encountered a blighted soul named Reginald of Falkenberg, once lord of a mighty castle that guarded the

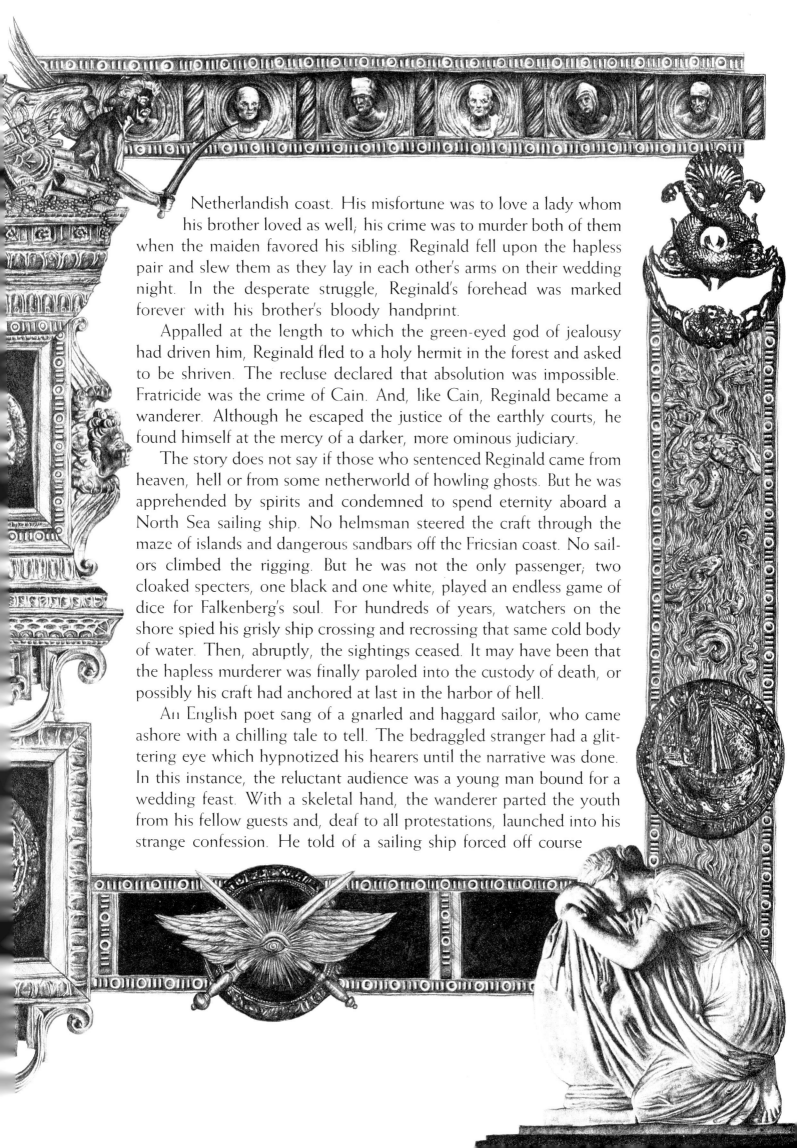

Netherlandish coast. His misfortune was to love a lady whom his brother loved as well; his crime was to murder both of them when the maiden favored his sibling. Reginald fell upon the hapless pair and slew them as they lay in each other's arms on their wedding night. In the desperate struggle, Reginald's forehead was marked forever with his brother's bloody handprint.

Appalled at the length to which the green-eyed god of jealousy had driven him, Reginald fled to a holy hermit in the forest and asked to be shriven. The recluse declared that absolution was impossible. Fratricide was the crime of Cain. And, like Cain, Reginald became a wanderer. Although he escaped the justice of the earthly courts, he found himself at the mercy of a darker, more ominous judiciary.

The story does not say if those who sentenced Reginald came from heaven, hell or from some netherworld of howling ghosts. But he was apprehended by spirits and condemned to spend eternity aboard a North Sea sailing ship. No helmsman steered the craft through the maze of islands and dangerous sandbars off the Friesian coast. No sailors climbed the rigging. But he was not the only passenger; two cloaked specters, one black and one white, played an endless game of dice for Falkenberg's soul. For hundreds of years, watchers on the shore spied his grisly ship crossing and recrossing that same cold body of water. Then, abruptly, the sightings ceased. It may have been that the hapless murderer was finally paroled into the custody of death, or possibly his craft had anchored at last in the harbor of hell.

An English poet sang of a gnarled and haggard sailor, who came ashore with a chilling tale to tell. The bedraggled stranger had a glittering eye which hypnotized his hearers until the narrative was done. In this instance, the reluctant audience was a young man bound for a wedding feast. With a skeletal hand, the wanderer parted the youth from his fellow guests and, deaf to all protestations, launched into his strange confession. He told of a sailing ship forced off course

by a terrible storm. Winds of unimaginable power drove the vessel steadily southward until it reached the drifting ice floes of the Antarctic seas. The crew were terrified by the absence of any sign of life. No seagulls wheeled above the masts, no fish leaped in the frigid waters. The only sounds were the creaking of the ice and the wind that wailed over it. Glittering icebergs moved to surround the ship and a thick blanket of fog dropped over it. Suddenly a bird flew out the mist. White as winter, and with a vast

wingspan, the albatross circled the craft and then perched atop the mast. Moments later the sky cleared and the ice broke up. The vessel was free again.

As the voyagers sailed northward into warmer waters, the albatross stayed with them, flying in their wake. The crew members, like all sailors, were superstitious. Some claimed the great bird had brought the fog. Others said the creature was a benign spirit who had come to their rescue.

The argument was resolved when one impulsive sailor took his crossbow and shot the bird. Its corpse fell with a

thud upon the deck and, at once, the winds died. The ship was becalmed. The sailors blamed the bowman, and hung the albatross's body around his neck as a token of shame. Tempers frayed; rations ran out. Hopes of rescue rose when a foreign craft hove into view, and fell again when the sailors saw it was a ghost ship, with two ghoulish figures playing dice on the empty deck. One by one, through thirst, disease and despair, the members of the crew began to die. As each seaman breathed his last, he turned

a baleful eye upon the comrade whose wanton act of violence upon the bird had brought down punishment on all their heads. Soon, only the man who had shot the albatross was left alive on the ship. He knew now, beyond any possible doubt, that it was no ordinary avian blood that he had shed. If the bird was not itself a god, it was at the very least a celestial messenger.

Avoiding the reproachful gaze of the staring corpses, the mariner waited for his own death and nourished himself on guilt and misery. Half delirious, he contemplated the wonders of

this unknown part of the ocean. Even in his wretchedness, he was moved by the strange beauty of a school of multicolored sea serpents, disporting in the clear waters. Unaccountably, the vision filled him with joy, and he blessed the water snakes as creatures of heaven. At that moment, the leaden weight of the albatross fell from his neck. The knots tied by the hands of his now-dead shipmates eased and loosened, and the feathered carcass slipped away from his body and dropped into the sea. But his strange adventures

were only just beginning. A troop of spirits took possession of the dead crewmen's corpses. Rising up, the unsouled bodies set to work. The sails suddenly billowed out with a wind that must have come from another world, and the ship moved on. With no apparent earthly navigator, the vessel traveled through uncharted seas and carried the lone sailor—entranced and terrified—safely back to the coastal waters of his native land.

When the ship was finally sighted, a pilot boat emerged from the harbor in order to guide it safely back into port.

As the smaller boat approached, the pilot and his companions perceived something uncanny: the complete silence on board the vessel, the apparent absence of a crew, an aura of doom that almost made them turn round and row in the opposite direction for all their lives were worth. But before the pilot could either flee or come any closer, a great turbulence cleaved the waters of the bay. A whirlpool sucked the death-ship down. The doomed craft sank without affording the pilot a single glimpse of its grisly crew.

Only the shocked but still living body of the sailor who had killed the albatross was found floating on the water. When he was rescued and brought ashore he could not rest until he had told his story, in lavish and meticulous detail, not once but a thousand times. There was no rest for him. He roamed the earth in search of new listeners. Whoever heard him was shaken from their careless complacency and transformed forever into a sadder and wiser soul. Thus, perhaps, did the mariner expiate the crime of destroying something that he did not understand.

# Chapter Three

# THE MEDIATORS

Aliens, said the old sages, walked often in our midst, agents dispatched into the world by unseen powers. They held in their hands the mechanisms of reward and retribution, carrying out the decrees of an implacable, unearthly court of law.

In the lore of many lands, these functions were fulfilled by angels. But they

were a far cry from the winged seraphs on stained-glass windows in the great cathedrals; they were lords of light, shape-shifters, terrifying in their powers.

Angels, however, were relatively new to the enchanted landscape. Far older, hot and angry as the molten earth at time's beginning, were the three Furies. Agents of the great Mother Goddess, these female avengers were at once beautiful and ghastly to behold. They stalked their victims through a walking nightmare, never failing to find them.

Other bearers of destruction or joy were nameless figures who appeared once to do their work and vanished forever. Cowled strangers were observed at scenes of disaster; inanimate objects, imbued with strange potencies, brought horror or delight; insects swarmed out of the underworld to avenge the dead. And behind all these mediators stood the Master of Chaos, that dark god of many names, an impresario of torments. Those cast out by higher powers became, by their license, his prey and his playthings.

# A Celestial Usurper

When the world was governed by the laws of magic, beings who were more than human walked the earth and used their uncanny powers to ensure that justice was done. They were discreet, even secretive, in their comings and goings, blending with the crowd or remaining invisible altogether until the moment came to impose a punishment or carry out a sentence on a sinner. Only then would they rear up and reveal themselves in all their terrible glory.

Sages and scholars might categorize them, according to their attributes, into the cohorts of a cosmic hierarchy, cogs in the mighty machine of justice. Poets named them spirits, daemons, messengers or jinn. But simpler folk called them angels and hoped they would never meet one. No one, however highborn, was exempt from their scrutiny, as a great Prince of Italy learned to his cost.

Many were the stories told of King Robert of Sicily. His heart was as cold as the marble that walled his palace. His arrogance bordered on the blasphemous: In his rare attendances at chapel, he yawned through the prayers and cantatas which praised a kingship higher than his own.

One day, while pursuing the pleasures of the chase in his game preserve, royal Robert met his comeuppance. Hot from hours of slaughtering deer and pursuing wild boar, he stripped off his garments to bathe in a stream. But when he emerged, refreshed, from the water, his servants and companions had vanished and his clothing had gone.

Naked and furious, he made his way back through the parkland to his palace and burst into the great hall. But the tongue-lashing he had been preparing for his seneschals died in his throat—for there, on the dais, absolutely identical to Robert in form and feature, sat another King, wearing his robes and his crown.

It took Robert a moment to comprehend the enormity of this imposture, for he had no way of knowing that it was an angel who had come to take his place, and that no one at court had noticed that anything was amiss. Recovering from the shock, Robert rushed up to his double and berated him.

"I am the King, and you have usurped my throne!"

The King's men-at-arms were about to punish this insolence when the angel restrained them.

"You are a fool," he told the intruder, "and henceforth you shall be my court jester. Let his head be shorn and give him a cap and bells as becomes his profession—and an ape to be his counselor." When Robert, still protesting, was led out between two burly guards, there was laughter among the courtiers and mock cries of "Long live the King!"

Thus began Robert's humiliating term of service. He slept on a bed of straw in the stables, with an ape as his only companion. Gradually he adjusted to his new role as the butt of every joke in the palace, but whenever the angel drew him aside to ask, half in jest, "Are you the King?" he would raise his head haughtily and reply, "Yes, I am the King."

After nearly three years had passed—

*An arrogant Sicilian King was punished for his pride by an angel,*
*who assumed the monarch's face and figure and usurped his throne. The*
*members of the royal court never noticed the difference.*

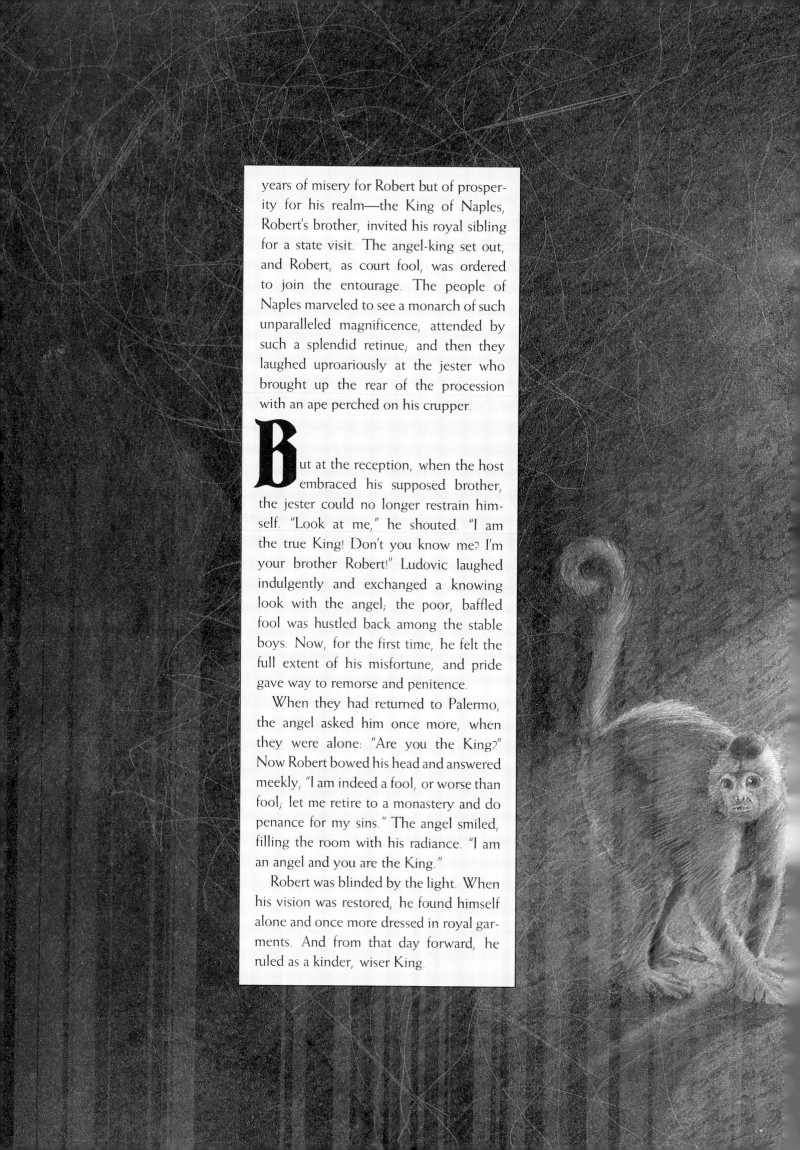

years of misery for Robert but of prosperity for his realm—the King of Naples, Robert's brother, invited his royal sibling for a state visit. The angel-king set out, and Robert, as court fool, was ordered to join the entourage. The people of Naples marveled to see a monarch of such unparalleled magnificence, attended by such a splendid retinue; and then they laughed uproariously at the jester who brought up the rear of the procession with an ape perched on his crupper.

But at the reception, when the host embraced his supposed brother, the jester could no longer restrain himself. "Look at me," he shouted. "I am the true King! Don't you know me? I'm your brother Robert!" Ludovic laughed indulgently and exchanged a knowing look with the angel; the poor, baffled fool was hustled back among the stable boys. Now, for the first time, he felt the full extent of his misfortune, and pride gave way to remorse and penitence.

When they had returned to Palermo, the angel asked him once more, when they were alone: "Are you the King?" Now Robert bowed his head and answered meekly, "I am indeed a fool, or worse than fool; let me retire to a monastery and do penance for my sins." The angel smiled, filling the room with his radiance. "I am an angel and you are the King."

Robert was blinded by the light. When his vision was restored, he found himself alone and once more dressed in royal garments. And from that day forward, he ruled as a kinder, wiser King.

# An Evil Loosed upon the World

The ancients believed that angels, like the one who taught Robert of Sicily his lesson in humility, watched over everyone, whether peasant or king. But angels also had a more sinister function, as Chên Hua-Fêng, a farmer in ancient China, discovered once long ago.

Chên was resting under a tree, watching his small herd of cows as they crowded together in a shady patch, flicking away the flies with their tails.

Suddenly he was aware of a figure moving toward him through the heat haze. Perhaps, thought Chên, he was a pilgrim, but why did he wear a thick scarf so high and tight around his neck when his face was pouring with sweat?

Chên invited the man to rest in the shade and suggested that he loosen the scarf. "Easy to loosen; hard to retie," was the stranger's answer as he sat down.

The pair whiled away the afternoon in conversation. The stranger hinted at travels across the mountains and up the Yangtze. Chên judged him to be a wise man when he also discussed the finer points of cattle. Chên brought from his store in a cave some of his best wine, wonderfully cool and in a fine jug. They drank one cup, and then another.

As dusk gathered, the stranger fell into a tipsy sleep. Chên was mystified to see a glow from his companion's head. Full of curiosity, he crept behind his guest to investigate, and furtively undid the scarf.

He was amazed to see that the source of the glow was a deep cavity in the back of the stranger's head, divided, like a honeycomb, into many cells, and covered with a layer of transparent skin. Horrified yet fascinated, Chên could not resist the temptation to draw from his jacket a pin and prod it into one of the cells to see what would happen. With a whispering sigh a small cow-like shape escaped, expanded and flew away.

The stranger awoke, furious. He was, he revealed, the Angel of Pestilence. He carried in his head every disease that assailed beasts and men. Chên had, in one act of folly, released cattle plague on the neighborhood.

Remorse and fear drove Chên to his knees to beg a remedy. Finally the angel named a powder which would effect a cure, but it would work only if Chên shared the knowledge with his neighbors. Then the stranger tightened his scarf and walked away into the twilight.

After three days all the cattle in the area began to lose their appetites. Their coats stood out from their bodies—a sign of plague. Chên told his brother, also a cattle owner, of the cure, but they kept it from their neighbors, hoping to profit by it. The brother's cattle soon recovered, but Chên's began to die. Only when his herd was reduced to five sickly cows did he heed the angel's warning.

He told his neighbors the remedy, and from that day his remaining cows, as well as those of his fellows, gathered strength. In time, his stocks increased and he knew prosperity once more.

# A Futile Flight from Retribution

The gods of Mount Olympus meted out justice to the Hellenic world with the same violence and passion shown by mortals. Their punishments for crimes of pride or impiety were fearful and final. Yet Greek chroniclers said that the most terrifying retribution was that delivered by agents of justice far older than Zeus or Athena—the three female spirits of vengeance named the Furies. Servants of the most ancient deity, Mother Earth, they were so feared that the storytellers themselves dared not say their names aloud.

In their dwelling-place at the western gateway to the underworld, the Furies heard all the cries of the dying. Amid the shrieks and screams, they listened above all else for one terrible cry: the curse of a mother murdered by the hand of her own child. This most hideous crime against their mistress Mother Earth drove the Furies up from the underworld, to hound the murderer to a death in agony and madness. One of the names they heard so cursed was Alcmaeon, Prince of Argos.

Alcmaeon had grown to manhood fatherless, raised on his mother's tales of her husband's death in war against Thebes. Yet, for all her stories of glory on the battlefield, the beautiful Eriphyle did not tell her son of his father's gift of prophecy, which had warned him against joining the doomed Theban campaign. Nor, in young Alcmaeon's presence, did she wear the shimmering robe with which another warrior, Polyneices, had bribed her. With this gift he had played on her vanity and encouraged her to undermine her husband's opposition to the war. Using all her wiles and charms, she had persuaded him to march to certain death in Thebes.

When Alcmaeon was tall and strong enough to wear his father's armor, the sons of other fallen heroes asked him to lead a second, vengeful war against Thebes. Like his father, Alcmaeon foresaw disaster and death. After days of indecision, he sought advice from his mother.

Eriphyle's clear and strong-willed eyes held his as she urged him to carry his father's sword into battle. While she spoke her stirring words of patriotism and glory, he noticed that she toyed with the strands of an amber necklace.

At his mother's bidding, Alcmaeon rode with his comrades at the head of the Argive army. Even as the people of Thebes saw the glint of helmets and shields advancing across the plain, their own Oracle foretold the fall of the city's walls. The Thebans fled that night, leaving their city to the Argives, who razed its walls and seized its treasure.

Back in his homeland, Alcmaeon continued to suffer disturbing dreams. Each one ended with the image of an amber necklace choking him. He would wake trembling, tearing at his throat.

One day, walking alone and troubled through the streets of Argos, he overheard his fellow soldier Thesander boasting of how he had lured Alcmaeon into the campaign. Thesander, like his father Polyneices, had bribed the vain Eriphyle to send her loved one into battle. He had tempted her with the gift of an amber necklace, just as Polyneices had done so years before with the shimmering robe.

Stunned, Alcmaeon rode at once to Delphi and consulted the Oracle. The voice of Apollo spoke to him, saying his mother deserved to die. In his grief and rage, Alcmaeon mistook this judgement for a command and returned to Argos and his mother's house. He burst into Eriphyle's bedroom where she was washing in a bowl of clear, sweet water. She screamed as he drew his dagger. Alcmaeon stabbed her in the throat and her dying curse came in strangled gasps:

"May the Holy Ones give you no peace, no resting-place, until my death is avenged."

The bowl darkened with his mother's blood, and Alcmaeon saw the ghastly forms of the Furies rising wraith-like from its vapors. As he watched in horror, the winged, sleek-bodied Furies transformed themselves into dog-faced devils with blood-red eyes. Their hair grew into nets of writhing snakes, forked tongues hissing. Alcmaeon fled from the brass scourges they wielded, and from the moans and wails of endless torment echoing in the air around them. He carried away with him the tokens of his mother's shame, the necklace and the robe.

With the Furies always at his back, he journeyed south to Psophis. There, King Phegus led him to the altar of Apollo and performed rites of purification to wash away his guilt. However, the servants of Mother Earth were not bound by Apollo's law. When the grateful Alcmaeon wed the King's daughter, giving her the necklace and the robe, the Furies caused the rich lands of Psophis to grow barren.

In desperation, Alcmaeon fled to the country of the river-god Achelous, where he said nothing of his stay in Psophis, nor of his wife there. In return for Alcmaeon's promise to wed his own daughter, the river-god created a delta of silt, new land outside the ancient domain of Mother Earth, where he could dwell in safety.

Though the Furies were unable to strike him directly there, they caused Alcmaeon's new bride to covet the necklace and robe left behind in Psophis. Unknowingly driven by the avengers, she tormented Alcmaeon about the gifts until at last he ventured from the safety of the delta and traveled back to Psophis. He did not tell King Phegus of his second marriage; instead, he explained that the Furies had agreed to forgive his crime in return for the consecration of the necklace and robe at the shrine of Apollo.

Eager for her husband to return to her free of torment, the King's daughter gladly gave up her gifts. That night, as Alcmaeon prepared to steal away, the Furies caused his servant to wander among King Phegus' men, speaking of his master's life on the river delta with his new bride. When King Phegus heard of this, he felt the rage of the Furies grow within him. He ordered his sons to kill Alcmaeon.

As the laughter of the Furies rang in his ears, Alcmaeon fell in his own blood on the dusty road from Psophis. When he had breathed his last, the three avengers sank back to the underworld whence they had come, to await the summons of another murdered mother's curse.

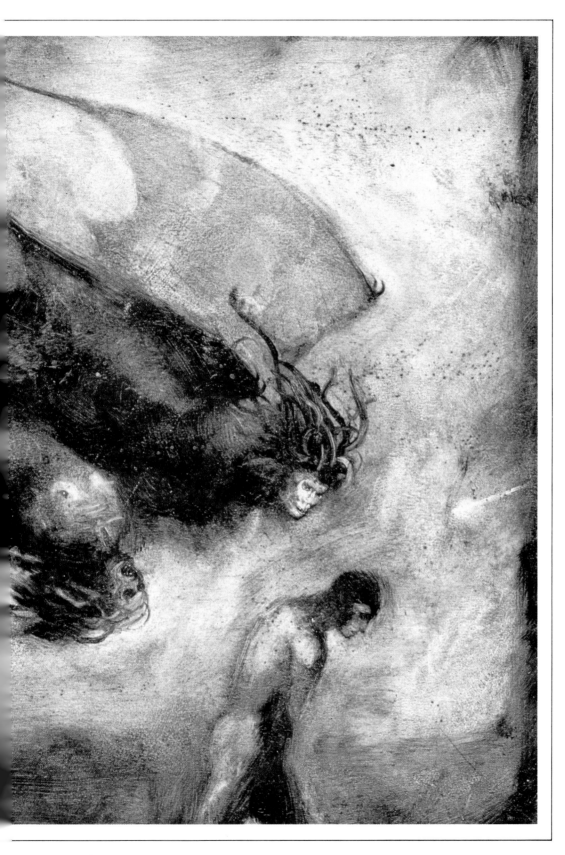

*Guilty of matricide, the Greek warrior Alcmaeon was hounded by the Furies, avenging spirits from the bowels of hell. Their intervention, and his own duplicity, led him into a fatal trap. In his death agonies, their triumphant shrieks rang in his ears until the darkness swallowed him.*

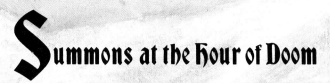

# Summons at the Hour of Doom

The raven flapping over the northern fields was often shunned as a creature of evil. It swooped on scuttling mice, plucked the eyes from newborn lambs, and followed hunters to feast on their kill. But the black bird was also revered as a mysterious messenger from the unseen powers that watched the world.

An Icelandic tale spoke of an incident when a raven held the threads of life and death in its beak. It happened in the far north of the island, where the farm Skidastadir huddled under the slopes of a grim, gray mountain.

The house was ruled by a miser, who gave his bondmen and maids just enough food to keep them alive and working. Bitterness infected the household. Its members were, in the main, as churlish as their master. They planted grudges and reaped quarrels.

Only one bondservant stood apart—a kitchen maid whose temperament had by some miracle remained untainted. She was a generous girl—secretly charitable to beggars and careful to save scraps from the table in the cold months for the birds and wild beasts that scavenged in the snow around the farm.

There came a winter so hard that animals died in the field and birds fell famished out of the sky. On an icy morning in January, the bondmaid found a half-starved raven on the threshold and nursed it back to strength with the scrapings of the pots. Once hale again, the bird returned to her each day at the hour when the northern sky was filled with flickering silver and lavender light. More than half tame, it would peck at the tiny portions of barley broth or porridge she held out in her ladle.

One afternoon, the bird appeared at the kitchen door but it refused the food it was offered. Instead it hopped three times around the ladle, flew a little way off,

then landed and hopped again, as if commanding the girl to follow.

Curious, the maid trailed after it, still holding out her ladle. The bird made a game of it and, by a combination of short hops and low flights, led her onward beyond the home paddock, well away from the farm. After a trek across the broad valley, the raven stopped short and lifted its head.

The girl followed its gaze to the ridge that loomed over Skidastadir. There, far above the slopes scarred with marks made by the plows of ancient farmers, she saw a white-robed stranger making his way upward through the scrub and over the rocks to the snow-covered mountaintop.

The figure paused, and seemed for a moment to look in her direction. Then he raised his staff and struck the rock face.

With a thundering that seemed to rumble out of the bowels of hell itself, the whole upper part of the mountain broke away. Millions of tons of stone, snow and frozen earth crashed down the slopes, destroying the farmhouse of Skidastadir and all who dwelled there. Only the bondmaid who had befriended the raven stood in a place of safety and survived to tell the tale.

# An Enchanted Snare for the Envious

In ancient China, learned philosophers taught that the nation was one vast family, with the Emperor at its head. Respect for one's relatives was the key to social harmony, for quarrels among kin could threaten the whole structure of society. Covetousness was especially to be avoided; the Chinese bards told a salutary tale of how a battered old chest sowed the seed of jealousy—and exacted the most terrible retribution.

On a summer's day many centuries ago, there was great rejoicing at the house of Li-Chuan, near the Yellow River. Three of his four sons were to marry—the eldest to the Emperor's daughter, the second to a general's daughter, and the third to the daughter of an important government minister.

Hundreds of guests had been invited to celebrate the family's good fortune. They gathered in the courtyard, wearing their finest silk robes; their splendid horses and carriages lined the road for a mile. But Li-Chuan's fourth son, Chang, was nowhere to be found. He too should have been married that day, with his brothers; but he had refused all the matches proposed to him by his father.

Yet on that very day, Chang fell in love. Wandering through the cherry orchards close to the river's edge, he met a young peasant girl. Her name was Feng and, in spite of her tangled hair and threadbare clothes, her beauty was unmistakable. At once, Chang asked her to be his bride. When Feng agreed, he hurried back to his father's house and summoned servants with a sedan chair, to carry his new bride home.

Although the wedding guests laughed secretly at Chang's humble bride, his father consented to the match. And so, all four brothers were married together, at one ceremony, and the feasting in the courtyard went on all day and lasted far into the night.

The next day, the four new wives took tea together, on the terrace of Li-Chuan's house. Each brought a jar of her favorite tea to share with the others. The Emperor's daughter had the finest tea of all: ginseng from Korea, famed for its beneficial powers. The General's daughter offered chrysanthemum tea, and the daughter of the Minister had orange-scented pekoe. But Chang's wife brought only the very cheapest green tea, and her sisters-in-law sneered, little dreaming that she had magic powers.

That night, when Chang entered his wife's room, he found her weaving a hobby horse out of straw.

"If I am to remain your wife," she told him softly, "you must ride to my father's house for a jar of tea."

And silencing his questions with her beautiful smile, she handed him the straw hobby horse. "Gallop down the Yellow River to the ocean and cross the surging waves to the lands beyond."

Despite his astonishment at Feng's strange request, Chang obeyed. The storytellers did not reveal the wonders of his journey, but at dawn he returned with a large jar of the most precious ginseng tea. Feng shared it with her three sisters-in-law and, as they

---

*Four Chinese sisters-in-law—three highborn, one a peasant wed above her station—exchanged gifts of tea.*

*Mocked by her wealthy kinswomen for offering commonplace green tea instead of rare ginseng or precious pekoe, the fourth woman soon revealed that she had magic powers far beyond their comprehension.*

marveled at its rich aroma, their contempt for Feng began to turn to envy.

Autumn faded slowly into winter. A
soft blanket of snow shrouded Li-Chuan's
house, and thick ice lay upon the lake.
Soon it was New Year's Eve. The wives
lighted incense in the frozen courtyard
and set off firecrackers to welcome the
New Year spirits. Since New Year was
traditionally a time for giving pres-
ents, the Emperor's daughter had
bought each of her sisters-in-law a
golden headdress sparkling with am-
ethysts, rubies and pearls. The General's daughter had

*When the time came for New Year's gift-giving, the humble bride astounded her husband's family by producing a mysterious coffer. Its battered exterior concealed a populous miniature city, filled with theaters, taverns, pleasure gardens and menageries.*

chosen three silk gowns; the daughter of the Minister had bought fine brocaded slippers in the latest Peking fashion.

But Feng had nothing to give to her sisters-in-law. So, early in the morning, she shook Chang awake and urged him to get dressed. "Go to the Yellow River," she said, "and fetch me the wooden box that is floating beside the bank." Chang slipped out of the house and ran down through the cherry orchard. When he came to the river, he found an old rotting tea-chest and carried it home to his wife.

That evening, the wives exchanged their New Year's gifts. The headdresses, gowns and slippers each caused gasps of delight. But the three senior wives sneered at Feng's battered old box, until she lifted the lid. And there inside was a vision beyond imagining: a miniature city, more wonderful than Peking itself, with temples and palaces, theaters and gardens, markets, shops and houses.

The wives called their husbands, and at a word from Feng the magic box grew so large that they all could enter and walk about the city, admiring the colored tiles shimmering on the temple roofs, and the peacocks strutting beside the fountains in the palaces. At one theater they watched Indian dancers sway with exquisite grace to the music of panpipes, drums and cymbals; at another, Mongolian acrobats swung from trapezes and vaulted through hoops. In the parks and gardens, gorgeous scents wafted across the evening air as flowers from every season bloomed at once. Elephants paced majestically across emerald lawns; hummingbirds hovered in the moonlight and parrots winked knowingly from monkey-puzzle trees.

As they wandered through markets, traders offered every luxury: perfumes from India, rubies from Ceylon, Sumatran spices and Siamese amber, Egyptian silver, Persian carpets, lapis lazuli from Samarkand and Turkestan jade. Then Feng led them to a restaurant that set out a tempting banquet: swallow's nest soup and snails in wine, crab's claws and shark's fins, carp with chestnut and wild duck with ginger, mushrooms, noodles, dumplings and exotic fruits.

At midnight the party left the restaurant, and the magic box gradually shrank in size until the guests could step back into Li-Chuan's house. Feng closed the lid and pushed the battered chest into the corner of her room. It was time to sleep, for the next day the Emperor, the General and the Minister would come to visit. But as their daughters lay in bed that night, they had already begun plotting to seize the box for themselves.

First to arrive was the Minister, in a smart carriage pulled by two plump horses snorting loudly in the frosty morning air. The General came next, galloping ahead of his escort—a squad of twenty cavalrymen sitting upright in the saddle, their rhinoceros-leather armor gleaming in the sunlight. At noon, trumpets announced the Emperor's approach. A bodyguard of fifty horsemen bearing pennants led the imperial carriage to Li-Chuan's gateway; footmen hurried from behind with a portable flight of steps for His Majesty to descend. Everyone knelt as the father of the Chinese nation stepped over Li-Chuan's threshold, wearing a magnificent yellow robe emblazoned with turquoise dragons.

But news of the wonderful magic box could not be delayed for a second. The Minister's daughter had already told the Minister; the General's daughter had informed the General. And now the Emperor's daughter darted to his side and whispered the fantastic story into her father's ear. An instant demonstration was commanded. But Feng was nowhere to be found. Her husband

120

was ordered to open the box himself. The Emperor gazed in wonder at the magic city revealed before his eyes.

Family ties were forgotten; the guests could think only of seizing the box for themselves. The Minister, urged on by his daughter, drew up an official proclamation banishing Li-Chuan and confiscating the contents of his home. The General scribbled an order to his aide, commanding the cavalrymen to surround the house. But the Emperor was more ruthless than either of them. At a drop of his wrist, the bodyguard sprang forward and butchered every person in the room. Only the Emperor's daughter was spared, and the two stood side by side gazing into the box, oblivious to the scene of bloodshed around them, enraptured by the magic world within.

Time stood still for them. They did not notice that outside the house winter was turning to spring with unnatural haste. The orchard was pink with cherry blossom, the snows were melting—and the Yellow River was rising dangerously fast. They did not hear the warnings of the imperial bodyguard, or hear the flood lapping at the courtyard wall. They did not feel the waters rising around their ankles, swirling steadily higher to embrace their waists and necks.

The magic box bobbed before their eyes until the Emperor and his daughter disappeared beneath the water. Then it was swept out of an open window and carried with the floods over the courtyard wall. It floated through the branches of the cherry orchard and back to the Yellow River, where Feng, in her old ragged cloak once more, watched from the bank. And, by nightfall, the fast-flowing current had carried it far away from land, into the surging waves of the China seas.

*Those who did not stop at murder to obtain the wonderful box learned their captured prize came complete with an unexpected punishment. Justice done, the coffer turned once more into a battered chest, mere flotsam drifting down the Yellow River toward the sea.*

# A Discriminating Distillation

A Japanese chronicle told of a kindly old man, known for his generosity, who dwelled below white-capped Mount Fuji. Sensing that his end was near, the ancient vowed he would die happy if he could taste one last cup of sake, the rice wine of his people. He begged his son, Koyuri, to obtain some. Koyuri was perplexed. He had no money to buy wine, and their only neighbor, Mimikiko, was a miser.

Unable to fulfill his parent's final wish, Koyuri wandered disconsolately along the shore with his empty gourd. A sudden ripple of mirth startled him. In the shade of a giant tree, he saw two extraordinary creatures lounging on the sand. Their long unruly hair was of the brightest red and their meager garments did little to hide their fat bellies and the curious pink hue of their flesh. Their faces were lined with laughter. A huge stone jar stood between them, and each held to his lips a large flat cup.

They asked the boy why he looked so downcast on such a joyous morning. When he told them of his sick father's longing, they rolled about in riotous laughter and pointed to the jar. It was full of the whitest, most fragrant rice wine Koyuri had ever seen. They filled his gourd to the brim.

At home, his father quaffed the precious liquid eagerly. Four days in succession, Koyuri returned for more. It was not greed which brought him back, he explained; the sake seemed to be restoring his father's health. The red-headed strangers gave without demur.

On the fifth day, as he returned with a full gourd, he was stopped by the miserly Mimikiko, who had watched his movements with growing curiosity. When Mimikiko heard about the miraculous sake, he demanded a taste. The boy handed him the gourd. Mimikiko sniffed the bouquet and his small eyes glittered. He raised the gourd to his lips. Then he gagged and spewed the liquid from his mouth, accusing Koyuri of trickery.

Koyuri offered to lead Mimikiko to the strangers and their sake. They welcomed him courteously and offered him drink. Yet, once again, he choked on the wine. Irate, he demanded an explanation.

The revelers grew serious as they explained that they were shojos, magical ocean-dwellers who attend on the great

*Pink-skinned and pot-bellied, shojos were the servants of the great sea dragon who ruled the waters around Japan. They were fond of the rice wine brewed by the gods, and cheerfully shared it with thirsty mortals. To virtuous humans the drink was nectar; to the wicked, a foul-tasting poison.*

sea dragon. Their sacred sake was sweet to those who were kind and generous. But it tasted vile to the cold-hearted Mimikiko. Even now, the poison was at work in his body. As cold sweat gathered on his brow and his stomach knotted in pain, Mimikiko promised to mend his ways if the shojos would spare him. Cruelty was not in their natures. They sprinkled a shimmering powder—an antidote—into his cup. Now the sake tasted delicious.

Mimikiko never forgot his promise; he became as open hearted as Koyuri and his father. In later days, they all built a hut together on the southern slopes of Mount Fuji. There they brewed the shojos' white sake and, drinking it daily, lived for three hundred years.

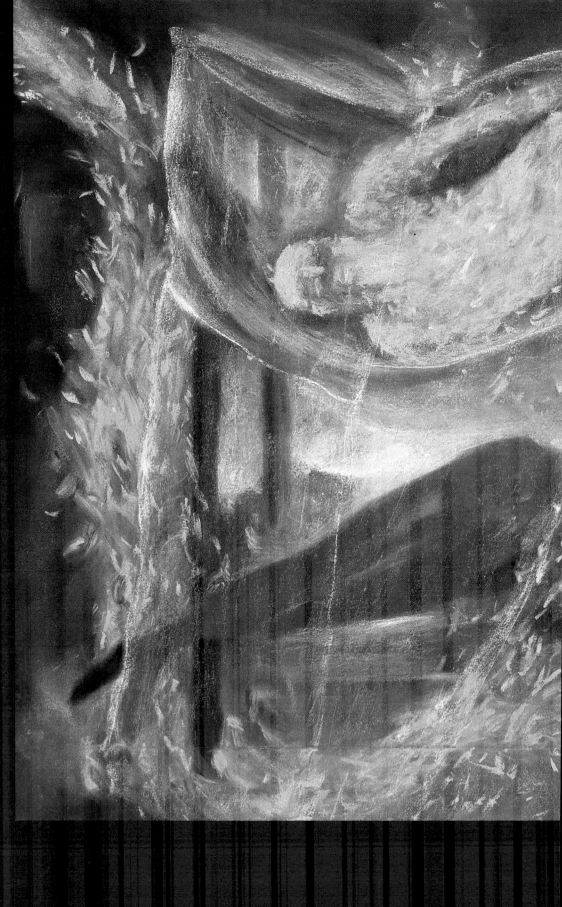

# The cold light
# of justice

The ancient sages knew that an injured soul could gather unto itself sufficient power to return from the grave and punish a persecutor. Every land had its tales of these angry revenants, and Japan, a country as abundant in ghosts as it was in cherry blossoms, had many accounts of posthumous revenge.

It was said that long ago, in Funakami village, there lived an old farmer named Kanshiro. A devout man, he traveled every summer to temples and holy places up and down the land. But there came a year when Kanshiro knew that winter had settled permanently in his bones. So he decided to make one final grand pilgrimage, to every important shrine in his homeland. Before he left his native village, Kanshiro's neighbors gave him a bag containing one hundred ryen, to offer to the Buddha on their behalf.

Kanshiro walked through intense summer heat for three days, until finally, feeling ill and unclean, he arrived at the village of Myojo, site of the great shrine of Ise, where even the rocks and trees were sacred. There he sought accommodation in a shabby inn.

The innkeeper, Jimpachi, listened as Kanshiro gasped out the story of his pilgrimage and of the money the villagers had given him for his devotions. His host reassured the old man that both he and his money were safe in the inn.

Kanshiro lay ill for five days, nursed by Jimpachi. On the morning of the sixth day he rose, ready to renew his journey. He thanked the innkeeper, who handed him his moneybag at the door.

Entering the shrine, the old man opened his sack to make a donation. The one hundred yen were gone, and in place of the coin was an equal weight of stones. Kanshiro hurried back to the inn.

Jimpachi screamed abuse at the old man and flung him out into the street. Kanshiro limped home to

make his shameful confession of the loss to his fellow villagers.

Most of the people of Funakami did not believe Kanshiro's story. Overcome by disgrace, he sold his small farm to refund his neighbors' money. With the pittance left, he resumed his last pilgrimage.

When he had prayed at every temple between the bleak northernmost reaches of Hokkaido and the warm shores of Kyushu in the south, he returned once more to the Ise shrine, in the village of Myojo.

Walking along its streets, he met the erstwhile innkeeper Jimpachi, now resplendent in the robes of a wealthy merchant. Kanshiro confronted his old enemy, accusing him of building his fortune on the coins he had stolen, and declared before the fascinated crowd of onlookers that he would be revenged.

At a nod from his master, one of Jimpachi's henchmen seized Kanshiro, beat him until he bled, and dragged him through the streets to the outskirts of the village. There the old man died. The next morning, the priests of the temple of Ise found Kanshiro's body and buried it in a small tomb.

That night, Jimpachi fell into a fever. As he lay delirious and paralyzed upon his sleeping mat, thousands upon thousands of fireflies streamed out the tomb of Kanshiro and through Jimpachi's window. They landed on the mosquito-net curtain that covered his bed. His screams alerted the household. But as quickly as his servants swatted the flies away, thousands more arrived.

Thicker and thicker grew the cloud of fireflies, until at last they tore a hole in the netting. Then they settled all over Jimpachi's body, filling his eyes, nose, ears, and mouth. Yet he did not die at once. His agony lasted for twenty days. Only then did the insects vanish.

The villagers knew that Kanshiro's spirit was now at rest, his honor satisfied.

# Stranger at the Revels

Sometimes an agent of punishment appeared in bland and unexpected guise, lulling his victims into false security before he revealed his true colors and struck them down. No one knew for certain what the sufferers saw in their last anguished moments of guilt, fear, and repentance come too late. But once the deed was done, a noisome whiff of brimstone lingered and the echoes of fiendish laughter took a long time to die away.

The gossips in the village of Stanton Drew, in England's green and rolling West Country, glanced warily over their shoulders when they remembered certain sinister events that took place on a June evening uncounted centuries ago. They told of a wedding party that began much like any other: a holy blessing for the couple, followed by an outdoor feast.

After the priest's solemnities were over, the bride and groom led friends and family through the fields to the banquet, which was spread out on long tables in the shadow of some ancient elms. The company ate apple cake dolloped with thick yellow cream, and drank themselves dizzy on strong cider. There were rude jokes and ribald toasts, sly winks and much merciless teasing by the groomsmen about the challenges a new husband would face on his wedding night.

After the wedding supper, the bride, bouncing with excitement, led a sequence of country dances. The village harpist plucked his strings to set the measure for their favorite round dances, reels, jigs, lavoltas and "strip the willow".

Barrel after barrel of cider was breached and the small progeny of the previous year's marryings squalled and grizzled until they fell asleep under the rough trestle tables. The rest of the party—wedded couples, bachelors and maids alike—kept on dancing, except for those furtive pairs who slipped away into the trees from time to time and came back, a long while later, hand in hand and smiling.

The light of the early summer evening lingered, but when it faded a great bonfire was lighted and the dancers' shadows grew long and leaping as they cavorted in its glow. But suddenly the harpist plucked one single sharp note and then silenced his instrument. The disappointed dancers stopped and cried out for more music.

The man shook his head. "No more this evening," he told them. He declared that it was past sunset and the holy Sabbath had begun. Everything had its hour and its seasons, and the sacred seventh day brought its own obligations. Now, he abjured his audience, was the time for rest and prayer, not revelry.

The dancers begged him not to be so unbending. The night was warm, the air soft and sweet, and the party just beginning. Someone noticed that his cup was empty, and filled it to the brim to encourage him to stay. He brushed it aside. Next they tried to persuade him with a bag of jingling silver, above the sum already given for his fee, but he shrugged and carefully bundled up his instrument. The groom cajoled him for just one more dance. The groomsmen alternately flattered and abused him, and the bridesmaids scolded, with arms akimbo and stamping

*Reveling the night away at a wedding, the villagers of Stanton Drew*
*never imagined that their riotous festivities would end in horror.*

feet. The bride, who had danced the hardest, grew petulant, then lost her temper altogether. She called the harper names and accused him of spoiling the celebrations that were supposed to mark the happiest day of her life.

The man remained steadfast. He was going home, he said, to sleep and say his prayers, and he advised the company to follow his example. The wedding guests drove him out of the elm grove with gibes and curses. The bride shouted after him that she would find another music-maker for her party if she had to go to hell itself.

No sooner had the harper set off along the path to the village than a stranger passed him, heading in the opposite direction, and approached the revelers. He asked why a bevy of young people, dressed in their finery, should be standing around with such miserable expressions.

They explained their plight, pointing to the distant figure of the departing harpist as he trudged home across the fields; they claimed that the wedding feast had

*The wheedling music cast a spell and forced the dancers into a*
*reel that never ended. Ignoring their pleas for a rest, the demonic piper played on.*

been ruined and the festivities cut off just as they were reaching their peak.

The newcomer smiled and said he had a remedy. He pulled out a pipe from under his cloak, made himself comfortable and launched into the tune for a lively reel. The crowd leaped up to dance. As his rhythms grew louder, their feet flew faster. Hours passed as minutes. Weird, frantic piping filled the grove and coaxed the dancers into strange steps and figures.

But when they finally grew tired and wished to rest, they found themselves unable to stop moving. The piper held them in an uncanny spell. Their faces contorted with fear and exhaustion; they begged the musician to release them. He merely smiled and played on.

Finally, the bonfire burned away to embers and the colors presaging morning streaked the sky. Over the keening of the pipe, the dancers heard the birds' dawn chorus. Then the first rays of the sun penetrated the elm trees and the piper put down his instrument at last.

The dancers collapsed. Then the bride screamed at the sight dawn revealed: the horns protruding from the stranger's head, the ebony edge of a cloven hoof, the gentle twitching of a pointed tail, the empty eyes. The Sabbath-breakers were transfixed with horror.

But even greater was the horror of their neighbors when, later that morning, they came in search of the missing revelers. For they found them in the elm grove, still in position for a round dance, but transformed into a circle of standing stones.

# PACHS TO A FINAL RECKONING

In a world dominated by dark forces, the lore of magical justice supplied the consoling image of an orderly universe. Many tales took as their subjects a pair of siblings—one good, one bad—who underwent a sequence of identical moral tests. The divergent ends of their parallel adventures displayed a pleasing and edifying symmetry.

The old Norse storytellers knew many variations on the theme. In one, the eternal duality was expressed by a pair of stepsisters. Of the two young women, one was sweet-tempered and industrious; the other—who yet could do no wrong in her mother's eyes—was indolent and spiteful. On a summer day warm enough to work outdoors, the two sat with their distaffs by the well. To pass the time they agreed to have a spinning contest. The one whose thread broke first would have to go down the shaft as a penalty.

Favoring her natural daughter, as always, the mother made sure that the unhandy girl had good flax to spin, while her nimble-fingered stepdaughter was given nothing but coarse bristles. Sure enough, it was not long before the girl's thread broke, despite all her skill. Bravely, she carried out her part of the bargain by climbing down the well shaft.

But it proved to be no ordinary well. It was, said the storytellers, a conduit to another

world altogether. When the girl stopped climbing, she found herself, unhurt, in a land of mountains and meadow. She set off to explore this unknown country, and soon discovered the alien nature that lay beneath its apparently ordinary landscape. First, she found her path barred by a hedge that spoke aloud, begging her to pass carefully, without damaging its foliage. Shocked but compliant, she slipped by, hardly disturbing a twig. The grateful hedge promised to help her if she should ever need it.

Next she met a brindled cow with a milking pail hung on its horn. To her amazement the cow asked her, in human speech, to milk it, which she willingly did. She drank from the milk at the cow's invitation—but only enough to slake her thirst.

As she went on her way she saw a great sheep choking with heat under its thick coat of wool. At its urgent request, she quickly and neatly sheared off its fleece with the clippers that hung from one horn.

She had not gone much farther when a laden apple tree pleaded to be relieved of the weight of its fruit. With a slender pole she found leaning against the tree, she carefully tapped down all the apples she could not reach. After eating a few, as the tree suggested, she laid the rest neatly at its foot.

Eventually she came to a large farm, where she turned in to ask for work to earn her keep. The house belonged to an old witch whose crabbed features and ominous mien marked her as a member of the tribe of trolls.

The witch set her a trio of tests: to fetch water in a sieve, to clean out a byre as big as a

meadow and, finally, to wash a black fleece white. Failure, she implied, would bring a punishment far too terrible to mention.

But if the witch brandished a sinister power, the heroine also found her own occult resources. Some swallows—honored in the old world as birds of luck and virtue—helped her to achieve her impossible tasks: putting clay in the sieve, sweeping with a magic broom, dipping the fleece in a butt of water that held enchantment.

To serve as payment for her work, the hag grudgingly offered her the choice of one of three caskets. The hovering birds made it plain through their liquid notes that this offer was not as straightforward as it seemed, and indicated which coffer the girl should choose. She seized the plainest of the three and fled, with the witch in pursuit, intending to kill her and reclaim the casket. But the creatures she had assisted earlier—the talking hedge, the cow, the sheep and the tree— each in turn supplied a hiding-place.

The chroniclers did not explain how, but she found and climbed the well again. Far from being glad to see her, her stepmother banished her to live in the pigsty. Once alone, she opened the casket. Soon she and her muddy quarters glittered with ropes of pearls, jeweled ornaments, garlands of gold and silver, and other treasures.

Furiously jealous, the stepsister determined to achieve the same good fortune. Accordingly, she descended the well and found herself in the green meadow. Identical tests awaited her, but she met them in a different mood. When she came to the hedge, instead

of heeding its plea to pass gently, she shoved her way rudely through, scattering and breaking the twigs. When she met the cow that needed milking, she drank the milk right up, and tossed the pail aside instead of hanging it neatly back on the cow's horn as her sister had done. And so it was with the sheep: She took the shears from its horn to clip the wool as it entreated, but did it so carelessly that she cut and tore its skin. The apple tree fared no better at her hands; she ate all the apples that she could easily reach, and then thrashed at the rest so roughly that she broke off whole branches and left the fruit as it lay on the ground.

When she reached the farm she could not at first persuade the witch to engage her. But she gracelessly refused to be put off, and at last the witch gave in. She was presented with exactly the same tasks as her sister, but her pride prevented her from heeding the helpful swallows. Irritably she pelted them with clay and stones to drive them away, and so lost any chance she might have had of coping with the witch's tasks.

At last, just to be rid of her, the witch offered her the choice of three caskets as wages for her work. The birds again gave their advice, telling her which to choose, but she took not the slightest notice of their kindly intervention. Instead, governed only by ignorance and acquisitiveness, she picked out the gaudiest, and set off home with it. She had no need to hurry or hide, for the witch was glad to see her go—and knew besides that she carried her punishment with her.

When the girl found her way back to the well and home again, she brandished the casket before her mother with a triumphant grin. But once they brought the box into the house and opened it, their avaricious glee turned to horror. For out of the coffer came not the precious gold and silver ornaments they had anticipated, but a loathsome, writhing tangle of bats and reptiles.

While her stepsister's quarters glistened with gems and treasure, her own chamber was soon beslimed with frogspawn, rodent droppings and sloughed-off snakeskins. And worse still, as the mother and daughter fell to mutual cursing and recriminations, it very soon became apparent that the girl could not open her mouth without a toad or a snake flopping out of it, so that no one, not even her formerly devoted parent, could bear the sight of her any longer.

# Acknowledgments

The editors wish to thank the following persons and institutions for their assistance in the preparation of this volume: Guy Andrews, London; Charles Boyle, London; Mike Brown, London; John Gaisford, London; Fred Grunfeld, Mallorca, Spain; Norman Kolpas, Los Angeles; Lea Lasko, Kensington and Chelsea Central Library, London; Caeia March, London; Robin Olson, London; Marian Smith Holmes, London; Christopher Spring, Museum of Mankind, London; The Tate Gallery, London; Deborah Thompson, London.

# Bibliography

Aldington, Richard, and Delano Ames, transl., *New Larousse Encyclopedia of Mythology*. London: The Hamlyn Publishing Group, 1985.

Andersen, Hans, *Fairy Tales*. Transl. by Mrs. H.B. Paull. London: Frederick Warne, no date.

Anderson, George K., *The Legend of the Wandering Jew*. Providence: Brown University Press, 1965.

Apollodorus, *The Library*. Transl. by Sir James George Frazer. London: William Heinemann, no date.

Armstrong, Edward A., *The Folklore of Birds*. London: Collins, 1958.

Arnason, Jón, *Icelandic Legends*. Transl. by George E.J. Powell and Eiríkur Magnússon. London: Longmans, Green, 1866.

Bain, R. Nisbet, ed. and transl., *Cossack Fairy Tales and Folk-Tales*. London: A.H. Bullen, 1902.

Baring-Gould, S., *Curious Myths of The Middle Ages*. London: Rivingtons, 1866.

Belgrave, M. Dorothy, and Hilda Hart, *Children's Stories from Indian Legends*. London: Raphael Tuck, no date.

Braun, Louis, W. Diez, and others, *Zur Geschichte der Kostüme*. Munich: Braun and Schneider, no date.

*Brewer's Dictionary of Phrase and Fable*. Revised by Ivor H. Evans. New York: Harper & Row, 1970.

Bryant, Sara Cone, *How to Tell Stories to Children*. Boston: Houghton Mifflin, 1924.

Bulfinch, Thomas, *The Golden Age of Myth & Legend*. London: Harrap, 1919.

Busk, R.H., *Sagas from the Far East*. London: Griffith and Farran, 1873.

Cavendish, Richard, ed., *Man, Myth and Magic*. 11 vols. New York: Marshall Cavendish, 1983.

Coleridge, S.T., *The Rime of the Ancient Mariner*. London: Hamilton Adams and Doré Gallery, 1876.

Cox, Marian Roalfe, *An Introduction to Folk-Lore*. London: David Nutt, 1895.

Dasent, Sir George Webbe, *Popular Tales from the Norse*. Edinburgh: David Douglas, 1903.

Davidson, Gustav, *A Dictionary of Angels*. New York: The Free Press, 1967.

Davidson, H.R. Ellis, *Gods and Myths of Northern Europe*. London: Penguin Books, 1964.

Davis, F. Hadland, *Myths & Legends of Japan*. London: Harrap, 1919.

Dillon, Myles, *Early Irish Literature*. Chicago: The University of Chicago Press, 1948.

Dirr, Adolf, *Caucasian Folk-Tales*. Transl. by Lucy Menzies. London: J.M. Dent, 1925.

Eberhard, Wolfram, *Chinese Fairy Tales and Folk Tales*. London: Kegan Paul, Trench, Trubner, 1937.

Eliade, Mircea, *Patterns in Comparative Religion*. Transl. by Rosemary Sheed. London: Sheed and Ward, 1958.

*Fairy-Tale Omnibus, The*. London: Collins, 1953.

Foote, Peter, and David M. Wilson, *The Viking Achievement*. London: Sidgwick & Jackson, 1970.

Gaster, Theodor H., *Myth, Legend, and Custom in the Old Testament*. London: Gerald Duckworth, 1969.

Gayley, Charles Mills, *The Classic Myths in English Literature and in Art*. Boston: Ginn, 1911.

Gibson, Michael, *Gods Men and Monsters from the Greek Myths*. London: Peter Lowe, 1977.

Giles, Herbert A., transl., *Strange Stories from a Chinese Studio*. London: T. Werner Laurie, 1916.

Gordon-Smith, Richard, *Ancient Tales and Folklore of Japan*. London: A. & C. Black, 1908.

Graves, Robert, *The Greek Myths*. Vols. 1 and 2. London: Penguin Books, 1960.

Griffis, W. E.:
*Japanese Fairy World*. London: Trübner, 1887.
*The Mikado's Empire*. New York: Harper & Brothers, 1900.

Grimm, Jacob and William, *Household Tales*. Transl. and ed. by Margaret Hunt. London: G. Bell & Sons, 1913.

Homer, *The Iliad of Homer*. Transl. by Samuel Butler, ed. by Louise R. Loomis. New York: Walter J. Black, 1942.

Hope, Thomas, *Costumes of the Greeks and Romans*. New York: Dover Publications, 1962.

Joly, H.L., *Legend in Japanese Art*. London: The Bodley Head, 1908.

Köhler, Carl, *A History of Costume*. Ed. by Emma von Sichart, transl. by Alexander K. Dallas. New York: Dover Publications, 1963.

Krappe, Alexander Haggerty, *The Science of Folk-Lore*. London: Methuen, 1930.

Leach, Maria, ed., *Funk & Wagnalls Standard Dictionary of Folklore, Mythology and Legend*. San Francisco: Harper & Row, 1984.

Longfellow, Henry Wadsworth, *The Poetical Works*. London: Frederick Warne, 1882.

Lowes, John Livingstone, *The Road to Xanadu*. London: Constable, 1930.

Macculloch, J.A., *The Childhood of Fiction: A Study of Folk Tales and Primitive Thought*. London: John Murray, 1905.

Macculloch, J.A., and Jan Máchal, *The Mythology of All Races: Celtic and Slavic*. Vol. 3. Boston: Marshall Jones, 1958.

Mackenzie, Donald A., *Myths of Babylon and Assyria*. London: The Gresham Publishing Company, 1915.

Magnus, Leonard A., *Russian Folk-Tales*. London: Kegan Paul, Trench, Trubner, 1916.

Marshall, Sybil, *Everyman's Book of English Folk Tales*. London: Everyman's Library, 1981.

Neugroschel, Joachim, transl., *Great Works of Jewish Fantasy*. London: Picador, 1978.

Oakes, Alma, and Margot Hamilton Hill, *Rural Costume*. London: B.T. Batsford, 1970.

Opie, Iona and Peter Opie, *The Classic Fairy Tales*. London: Oxford University Press, 1974.

Ovid, *The Metamorphoses*. Transl. by Mary M. Innes. London: Penguin Books, 1955.

Peppin, Brigid, *Fantasy*. New York: New American Library, 1976.

Piggott, Juliet, *Japanese Mythology*. Feltham: Newnes Books, 1984.

Power, Rhoda, *How it Happened*. Cambridge: Cambridge University Press, 1930.

Rolleston, T.W., *Myths & Legends of the Celtic Race*. London: Harrap, 1911.

Rose, H.J., *A Handbook of Greek Mythology*. London: Methuen, 1928.

Ross, Anne, *Druids, Gods and Heroes from Celtic Mythology*. London: Peter Lowe, 1986.

Rubens, Alfred, *A History of Jewish Costume*. London: Weidenfeld and Nicolson, 1973.

Sanders, Nancy Katharine, *The Epic of Gilgamesh*. London: Penguin Books, 1960.

Sanders, Tao Tao Liu, *Dragons, Gods & Spirits from Chinese Mythology*. London: Peter Lowe, 1980.

Seignobos, Charles, *The World of Babylon*. Transl. by David Macrae. New York: Leon Amiel, 1975.

Skinner, Charles Montgomery, *Myths and Legends of Flowers, Trees, Fruits, and Plants*. Philadelphia: J.B. Lippincott, no date.

Thompson, Stith:
*The Folktale*. New York: The Dryden Press, 1951.
*Motif-Index of Folk-Literature*. 5 vols. Bloomington: Indiana University Press, 1968.

Untermeyer, Louis, ed., *The Albatross Book of Living Verse*. London: Collins, no date.

Webster, T.B.L., *Everyday Life in Classical Athens*. London: B.T. Batsford, 1969.

Werner, E.T.C.:
*A Dictionary of Chinese Mythology*. New York: The Julian Press, 1961.
*Myths & Legends of China*. London: Harrap, 1924.

Williams, C.A.S., *Outlines of Chinese Symbolism and Art Motives*. Rutland, Vermont: Charles E. Tuttle Company, 1981.

Williams, Harcourt, *Tales from Ebony*. London: Putnam, 1934.

Williams, Mary Wilhelmine, *Social Scandinavia in the Viking Age*. New York: Macmillan, 1920.

# Picture Credits

Time-Life Books Inc.
is a wholly owned subsidiary of

# TIME INCORPORATED

FOUNDER: Henry R. Luce 1898-1967

*Editor-in-Chief:* Henry Anatole Grunwald
*President:* J. Richard Munro
*Chairman of the Board:* Ralph P. Davidson
*Corporate Editor:* Ray Cave
*Group Vice President, Books:* Reginald K. Brack Jr.
*Vice President, Books:* George Artandi

## TIME-LIFE BOOKS INC.

EDITOR: George Constable
*Director of Design:* Louis Klein
*Director of Editorial Resources:* Phyllis K. Wise
*Acting Text Director:* Ellen Phillips
*Editorial Board:* Russell B. Adams Jr.,
Dale M. Brown, Roberta Conlan,
Thomas H. Flaherty, Donia Ann Steele,
Rosalind Stubenberg, Kit van Tulleken,
Henry Woodhead
*Director of Photography and Research:* John
Conrad Weiser

EUROPEAN EDITOR: Kit van Tulleken
*Assistant European Editor:* Gillian Moore
*Design Director:* Ed Skyner
*Chief of Research:* Vanessa Kramer
*Chief Sub-editor:* Ilse Gray

PRESIDENT: Reginald K. Brack Jr.
*Executive Vice Presidents:* John M. Fahey Jr.,
Christopher T. Linen
*Senior Vice Presidents:* James L. Mercer,
Leopoldo Toralballa
*Vice Presidents:* Stephen L. Bair, Ralph J.
Cuomo, Neal Goff, Stephen L. Goldstein,
Juanita T. James, Hallett Johnson III, Robert
H. Smith, Paul R. Stewart
*Director of Production Services:* Robert J.
Passantino

## THE ENCHANTED WORLD

SERIES DIRECTOR: Ellen Galford
*Picture Editor:* Mark Karras
*Designer:* Mary Staples
*Series Secretary:* Eugénie Romer

Editorial Staff for *Magical Justice*
*Researcher:* Lesley Coleman
*Sub-editor:* Frances Dixon
*Assistant Designer:* Julie Busby

Editorial Operations
*Copy Chief:* Diane Ullius
*Editorial Operations:* Caroline A.
Boubin (manager)
*Production:* Celia Beattie
*Quality Control:* James J. Cox (director)
*Library:* Louise D. Forstall

Correspondents: Elisabeth Kraemer-Singh
(Bonn); Dorothy Bacon (London);
Maria Vincenza Aloisi (Paris); Ann
Natanson (Rome).

## Chief Series Consultant

Tristram Potter Coffin, Professor of
English at the University of Pennsylvania, is a leading authority on folklore.
He is the author or editor of numerous
books and more than one hundred articles. His best-known works are *The British Traditional Ballad in North America, The
Old Ball Game, The Book of Christmas Folklore* and *The Female Hero.*

This volume is one of a series that is based
on myths, legends and folk tales.

*Other Publications:*

SUCCESSFUL PARENTING
HEALTHY HOME COOKING
UNDERSTANDING COMPUTERS
YOUR HOME
THE KODAK LIBRARY OF CREATIVE PHOTOGRAPHY
GREAT MEALS IN MINUTES
THE CIVIL WAR
PLANET EARTH
COLLECTOR'S LIBRARY OF THE CIVIL WAR
THE EPIC OF FLIGHT
THE GOOD COOK
WORLD WAR II
HOME REPAIR AND IMPROVEMENT
THE OLD WEST

For information on and a full description
of any of the Time-Life Books series listed
above, please write:
Reader Information
Time-Life Books
541 North Fairbanks Court
Chicago, Illinois 60611

Library of Congress Cataloguing in
Publication Data
Magical justice.
   (The Enchanted world)
   Bibliography: p.
   1. Justice – Folklore. 2. Tales.
3. Mythology.
I. Time-Life Books.    II. Series.
GR877.M34 1986       398.2'7       86-14530
ISBN 0-8094-5269-3
ISBN 0-8094-5270-7 (lib. bdg.)

Time-Life Books Inc. offers a wide range of
fine recordings, including a *Big Bands* series.
For subscription information, call 1-800-621-
7026 or write TIME-LIFE MUSIC, Time &
Life Building, Chicago, Illinois 60611.

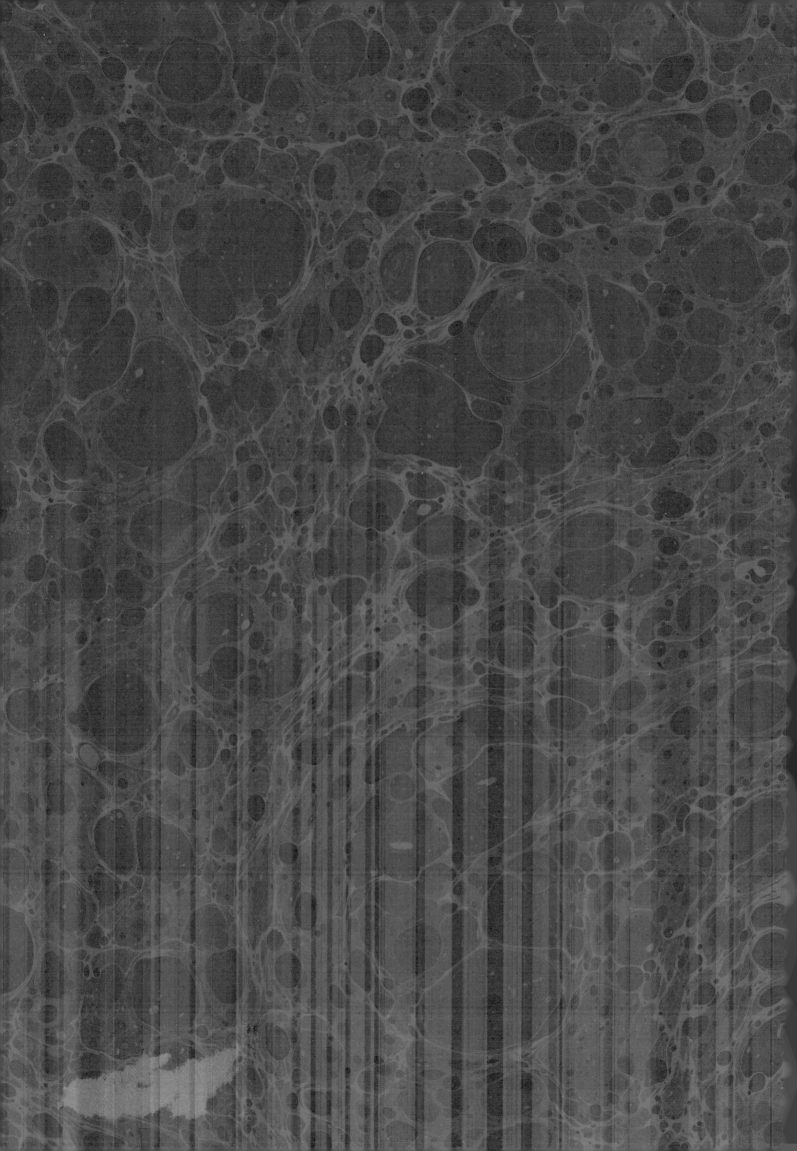